Copyright

Sustainable Finance, ESG, Impact Investing, and Carbon Markets: Financing the Global Transition to a Low-Carbon, Climate-Resilient Economy

The author and publisher are of the same opinion regarding the views and content expressed in this work.

Disclaimer: The information in this book is provided for general knowledge and educational purposes only. While every effort has been made to ensure accuracy, the author and publisher make no representations or warranties with respect to the completeness or suitability of the content. The author and publisher accept no liability for any errors, omissions, or outcomes resulting from the application of information contained herein. Readers are advised to consult appropriate professionals or authorities before acting on any material presented.

ISBN (eBook): 978-1-991368-98-0
ISBN (Paperback): 978-1-991368-99-7

Published by Global Climate Solutions
First Edition, 2026
Cover design and interior layout by Global Climate Solutions

Table of Contents

Introduction

The transition to a low-carbon, climate-resilient economy is, in its practical detail, a financing problem. The technologies required to halve global emissions by 2030 exist across every major sector, and the constraint on deploying them is rarely conceptual (IPCC, 2022). It is a question of how much capital moves, how quickly it moves, where it moves to, and what return it demands along the way. That question sits at the center of this book.

The headline numbers suggest a system already in motion. Global energy investment is set to reach USD 3.3 trillion in 2025, with roughly USD 2.2 trillion flowing to renewables, nuclear, grids, storage, efficiency, and electrification against USD 1.1 trillion for oil, gas, and coal (IEA, 2025). Global climate finance reached an all-time high of USD 1.9 trillion in 2023 (Climate Policy Initiative, 2025). Measured as aggregate volume, capital reallocation is underway.

The composition of those flows tells a less reassuring story. Adaptation attracted only USD 65 billion in 2023, a fraction of mitigation finance, because adaptation rarely generates the contracted revenue stream that private capital requires (Climate Policy Initiative, 2025). Africa accounts for 2 percent of global clean energy investment while holding 20 percent of the world's population, and energy investment across the continent is lower in real terms than it was a decade ago (IEA, 2025). The binding constraint in most of these markets is not the absence of viable projects or the global availability of savings. It is the cost of capital, which varies so sharply across jurisdictions that identical technologies produce entirely different investment outcomes depending on where they are built (Ameli et al., 2021).

This book treats sustainable finance not as a product category or an asset class but as a set of institutional mechanisms that determine where capital goes and at what price. Those mechanisms fall into three broad families. Disclosure rules and classification systems attempt to correct information problems so that climate risk is priced. Instruments and intermediation structures, including labeled debt, impact funds, and concessional capital, attempt to change the risk-return profile of specific transactions. Carbon pricing attempts to correct the underlying externality directly. Each family rests on different assumptions, carries different evidence standards, and succeeds or fails for different reasons.

The argument develops in sequence. Chapter 1 establishes the conceptual framework and the economic logic that justifies intervention in capital allocation. Chapters 2 and 3 examine the regulatory and analytical infrastructure built around information: disclosure regimes, taxonomies, ESG ratings, and portfolio integration. Chapters 4 through 6 turn to the instruments that actually move capital, covering labeled debt markets, impact investing, and blended finance in emerging economies. Chapters 7 and 8 address carbon pricing in its compliance and voluntary forms. Chapter 9 examines what existing mechanisms fail to reach, including transition finance for heavy industry, adaptation, and nature.

The analysis throughout distinguishes mechanisms that change the cost and direction of capital from those that primarily change measurement and reporting. That distinction, more than any headline figure, determines whether the machinery assembled over the past decade is equal to the task it was built for.

References

Ameli, N., Dessens, O., Winning, M., Cronin, J., Chenet, H., Drummond, P., Calzadilla, A., Anandarajah, G., & Grubb, M. (2021). Higher cost of finance exacerbates a climate investment trap in developing economies. Nature Communications, 12(1), 4046. https://doi.org/10.1038/s41467-021-24305-3

Climate Policy Initiative. (2025). Global Landscape of Climate Finance 2025. Climate Policy Initiative.

https://www.climatepolicyinitiative.org/publication/global-landscape-of-climate-finance-2025/

IEA. (2025). World Energy Investment 2025. IEA. https://www.iea.org/reports/world-energy-investment-2025

IPCC. (2022). Climate Change 2022: Mitigation of Climate Change. IPCC. https://www.ipcc.ch/report/ar6/wg3/

Chapter 1: The Architecture of Sustainable Finance

Sustainable finance is often described as though it were an asset class, a product range, or a category of investor. It is more accurately understood as a set of institutional mechanisms for redirecting capital, assembled over roughly two decades in response to a specific economic problem. This chapter sets out that problem, the logic that justifies intervention in capital allocation, and the structural features of financial markets that determine how quickly capital can move. It then distinguishes the principal strands of the field and explains how they relate to one another, establishing the vocabulary and analytical structure the remainder of the book depends on.

Defining Sustainable Finance and Its Boundaries

Definitions of sustainable finance vary across regulatory, institutional, and market usage, and the variation is consequential rather than semantic. In its broadest regulatory framing, sustainable finance covers any financial activity that incorporates environmental, social, and governance considerations into investment or lending decisions. Narrower definitions restrict the term to capital directed at activities that make a measurable contribution to environmental objectives. The difference determines what can be counted, what can be labeled, and what can be regulated.

The choice between them is not neutral. A broad definition produces large reported volumes and a correspondingly weak claim about what those volumes accomplish, since most capital in a diversified portfolio can be described as ESG-integrated without changing what the portfolio holds. A narrow definition produces small volumes and a stronger claim, but it excludes the emissions-intensive activities where the largest abatement opportunities sit. Neither framing is dishonest, yet the two support very different conclusions about progress.

Several adjacent concepts overlap without being synonymous. Climate finance typically refers to flows supporting mitigation and adaptation, often in a development or treaty context. Green finance describes capital directed at environmentally beneficial activity. Transition finance addresses activities that are currently emissions-intensive but moving toward alignment. Responsible investment describes a process rather than an outcome, covering the integration of non-financial factors into analysis regardless of where capital ultimately lands.

A more fundamental distinction cuts across all of these. Investors pursue sustainability objectives for two quite different reasons, and conflating them produces persistent confusion about what the field is for. Value-based motivations treat environmental and social factors as financially material information bearing on risk and return. Values-based motivations reflect preferences that investors are willing to accept financial trade-offs to express. These rationales generate different testable implications, and much of the disagreement about whether sustainable investing "works" reflects a failure to specify which claim is being evaluated (Starks, 2023).

Definitional imprecision has practical consequences. It determines the reported size of sustainable fund markets, the scope of disclosure obligations, and the criteria against which greenwashing claims are assessed. A fund that screens out a handful of tobacco and weapons producers and a fund that finances new transmission infrastructure can both be described as sustainable under permissive definitions, though they do entirely different things to the physical economy. When the market is sized by adding them together, the resulting figure measures the popularity of a label rather than the volume of capital doing anything in particular.

The boundary problem also shapes who bears the cost of compliance. Broad definitions capture large numbers of financial products and impose reporting obligations across most of an asset management industry. Narrow definitions concentrate obligations on a smaller set of explicitly labeled products while leaving the majority of capital untouched. Neither approach is obviously correct, and jurisdictions have resolved the trade-off differently. Much of the regulatory architecture examined in Chapter 2 exists to impose boundaries where market usage had left them open.

The Market Failure Logic of Capital Reallocation

The economic case for intervening in capital allocation rests on identifiable market failures rather than on ethical assertion. The primary failure is an unpriced externality: greenhouse gas emissions impose costs on parties who are not participants in the transaction generating them. Absent a price on those emissions, private returns diverge systematically from social returns, and capital flows toward emissions-intensive assets in volumes that would not survive full cost accounting.

A second failure concerns information. Climate-related risks are unevenly disclosed, inconsistently measured, and difficult to attribute to individual assets. Investors cannot price what they cannot observe, and the resulting information asymmetry allows mispricing to persist. Most of the disclosure architecture built over the past decade addresses this problem directly, on the assumption that better information produces better pricing.

That assumption warrants scrutiny. Climate-related financial risks are characterized by radical uncertainty rather than by calculable probability distributions, which means efficient price discovery may not be achievable regardless of disclosure quality. Market-based corrections including disclosure, scenario analysis, and stress testing address perceived information gaps, but they are limited where the underlying risk is genuinely unknowable rather than merely unmeasured. This framing also biases policy toward avoiding short-term market disruption at the expense of long-term, potentially irreversible outcomes, and it supports a precautionary approach that integrates climate risk into prudential, macroprudential, and monetary policy frameworks (Chenet et al., 2021).

A third failure is temporal. Climate risks materialise over decades, while investment mandates, performance evaluation, and compensation operate over quarters and years. This horizon mismatch means that risks which are material to an asset may be immaterial to the person choosing to hold it. A portfolio manager evaluated on three-year relative performance has little reason to act on a repricing expected in 2040, even when convinced it will occur. The mismatch is structural rather than a failure of individual judgment, which is why exhortation to think long term has produced so little observable change in allocation.

A fourth failure concerns coordination. Many low-carbon assets depend on complementary infrastructure that no single investor can provide. Electric vehicle charging networks, grid interconnection, hydrogen transport, and port facilities for offshore wind all exhibit returns that depend on other parties investing simultaneously. Each participant rationally waits for the others, and the resulting equilibrium leaves profitable investments unmade. This is a classic coordination problem rather than an information or pricing problem, and neither disclosure nor carbon pricing addresses it directly.

Disclosure, pricing, and concessional intervention represent the three principal corrective mechanisms available. Each addresses a different failure, and the frequent assumption that they are substitutes for one another accounts for a good deal of disappointment about their individual performance.

The Scale and Composition of the Investment Requirement

Estimates of the investment required to meet climate objectives are constructed in different ways, and the differences matter more than the headline figures. Gross investment requirements describe total capital deployment in energy systems and infrastructure. Net incremental costs describe the additional expenditure relative to a counterfactual in which the same services are delivered through conventional technology. The two can differ by an order of magnitude, and conflating them overstates the fiscal and financial challenge considerably.

Sectoral coverage introduces a further source of divergence. Energy system estimates are comparatively tractable because technologies, costs, and capacity requirements can be modeled explicitly. Estimates covering industry, buildings, agriculture, and land use rest on weaker foundations, and adaptation investment is harder still to quantify because the benefit is an avoided loss rather than a delivered service. Aggregate figures that combine these categories inherit the uncertainty of their weakest component, which is rarely visible in the way the totals are presented and debated.

Current flows provide a baseline. Global energy investment is set to reach USD 3.3 trillion in 2025, of which roughly USD 2.2 trillion goes to renewables, nuclear, grids, storage, low-emissions fuels, efficiency, and electrification, against USD 1.1 trillion for oil, natural gas, and coal. Solar alone is expected to account for USD 450 billion, the single largest line item in global energy investment (IEA, 2025). Options to at least halve emissions by 2030 exist across all sectors, which locates the constraint in deployment rather than in technological availability (IPCC, 2022).

The geographic distribution of those flows is where the gap becomes visible. Africa accounts for 2 percent of global clean energy investment while holding 20 percent of the world's population, and total energy investment across the continent is one-third lower in 2025 than it was in 2015 (IEA, 2025). This is not a shortfall in global savings. Aggregate capital availability is not the binding constraint in most markets; the binding constraint is the terms on which that capital is willing to be deployed in particular jurisdictions.

The mechanism behind that constraint is the cost of capital. Modeling decarbonization pathways with region-specific weighted average cost of capital rather than a uniform global assumption produces 35 percent lower green electricity production in Africa on a cost-optimal 2°C pathway, and policy interventions that lower financing costs for low- and high-carbon technologies alike would allow the region to reach net zero roughly a decade earlier. Where climate-related investment remains chronically insufficient because financing costs are high, and financing costs remain high because investment is insufficient, the result is a self-reinforcing climate investment trap (Ameli et al., 2021).

That distinction reframes the problem. Where capital is abundant and cheap, the investment gap is largely a question of project pipeline and policy certainty. Where capital is scarce and expensive, the gap is a question of risk pricing, and no amount of disclosure or labeling will close it.

Capital Structures, Intermediaries, and Allocation Channels

Capital reaches low-carbon assets through a chain of intermediaries, each operating under constraints that determine what it can hold. Asset owners, including pension funds and insurers, hold long-dated liabilities and can in principle match them with long-dated assets, but they face liquidity requirements and fiduciary obligations that limit exposure to illiquid or unrated instruments. Asset managers operate against benchmarks and mandates set by others. Banks face risk-weighting rules that price capital consumption against asset characteristics. Development finance institutions and public budgets operate under different objectives entirely.

Instrument design must match the constraints of the intended capital provider, and much of the innovation examined in later chapters consists of repackaging the same underlying cash flows into forms different intermediaries can hold. A project that a development bank can lend against directly may need to be aggregated, rated, and securitised before an institutional investor can hold it. The economic substance is unchanged by this repackaging; what changes is whether a given pool of capital is permitted to participate.

This helps explain why headline commitments from large asset owners translate poorly into deployed capital. An institution managing long-dated liabilities may genuinely intend to increase infrastructure exposure, but its internal risk framework may permit only rated instruments above a minimum issue size with an established secondary market. Individual renewable projects in smaller markets satisfy none of those conditions. The capital is willing and the projects are viable, yet no permissible instrument connects them. Closing that gap is an engineering problem in financial structuring rather than a question of investor intent.

These intermediation chains also determine where risk ultimately settles, which is frequently not where it appears to originate. Tracing equity risk from 43,439 oil and gas production assets through a global network of 1.8 million companies shows that global stranded assets, measured as the present value of lost future upstream profits, exceed USD 1 trillion under plausible changes in climate policy expectations. Most of that market risk falls on private investors overwhelmingly based in OECD countries, including substantial exposure held through pension funds, and the ownership structure produces an international net transfer of more than 15 percent of global stranded asset risk to OECD-based investors (Semieniuk et al., 2022).

The policy instruments operating on these channels have uneven records. Across nine categories of climate finance policy, feed-in tariffs, tax credits, loan guarantees, and national development banks show demonstrable effectiveness at mobilizing private capital, while evidence on disclosure policies, targeted lending, national climate funds, and green bonds remains weak or thin (Bhandary et al., 2021).

The Analytical Strands of the Field and How They Connect

The mechanisms examined in this book pursue different objectives and rest on different evidence standards. ESG integration treats sustainability factors as inputs to conventional risk and return analysis, and its success criterion is improved risk-adjusted performance or better-informed pricing. Impact investing asserts a causal claim about real-world outcomes, and its success criterion is additionality that would not have occurred otherwise. Labeled debt markets attempt to direct proceeds or condition pricing on performance. Blended finance uses concessional capital to alter the risk-return profile of transactions that would not otherwise proceed. Carbon pricing corrects the externality directly, without relying on investor preference at all.

These logics can conflict within a single portfolio. An investor pursuing portfolio decarbonization through divestment reduces measured financed emissions without necessarily reducing emissions anywhere in the real economy. An investor pursuing additionality may need to increase exposure to high-emitting assets precisely so their transformation can be financed. Both investors can report progress against their stated objective while moving in opposite directions, and the two objectives can be pursued simultaneously only if the difference between them is stated explicitly rather than blurred under a common label.

The mechanisms also differ in how much they depend on voluntary participation. ESG integration, impact investing, and labeled debt all require someone to choose them, which caps their reach at the share of capital whose owners are willing to act. Carbon pricing and prudential regulation apply regardless of preference. This distinction largely determines the ceiling on each mechanism's effect: voluntary approaches are constrained by the wealth share of participating investors, while mandatory ones are constrained only by political durability. Much of the empirical disappointment surrounding voluntary mechanisms follows from expecting preference-driven capital to accomplish what only universal application can.

The literature assessing these mechanisms carries a structural weakness worth noting at the outset. Across asset stranding studies, model-based transition risk assessment, and financial empirics of the low-carbon transition, the proliferation of competing methods hampers comparison of results and integration of research designs, making it difficult to form a synthetic view or to identify which uncertainties remain genuinely unresolved (Daumas, 2023). Claims about what sustainable finance has achieved should be read with that limitation in mind.

The distinction that organises the chapters ahead is therefore not between instruments but between functions. Some mechanisms change the information available about capital. Others change the cost or availability of capital for specific activities. Others change the relative economics of emitting. Only the second and third categories alter allocation directly, and separating them from the first is the analytical task the rest of this book undertakes.

References

Ameli, N., Dessens, O., Winning, M., Cronin, J., Chenet, H., Drummond, P., Calzadilla, A., Anandarajah, G., & Grubb, M. (2021). Higher cost of finance exacerbates a climate investment trap in developing economies. Nature Communications, 12(1), 4046. https://doi.org/10.1038/s41467-021-24305-3

Bhandary, R. R., Gallagher, K. S., & Zhang, F. (2021). Climate finance policy in practice: a review of the evidence. Climate Policy, 21(4), 529-545. https://doi.org/10.1080/14693062.2020.1871313

Chenet, H., Ryan-Collins, J., & van Lerven, F. (2021). Finance, climate-change and radical uncertainty: Towards a precautionary approach to financial policy. Ecological Economics, 183, 106957. https://doi.org/10.1016/j.ecolecon.2021.106957

Daumas, L. (2023). Financial stability, stranded assets and the low-carbon transition – A critical review of the theoretical and applied literatures. Journal of Economic Surveys, 38(3), 601-716. https://doi.org/10.1111/joes.12551

IEA. (2025). World Energy Investment 2025. IEA. https://www.iea.org/reports/world-energy-investment-2025

IPCC. (2022). Climate Change 2022: Mitigation of Climate Change. IPCC. https://www.ipcc.ch/report/ar6/wg3/

Semieniuk, G., Holden, P. B., Mercure, J. F., Salas, P., Pollitt, H., Jobson, K., Vercoulen, P., Chewpreecha, U., Edwards, N. R., & Viñuales, J. E. (2022). Stranded fossil-fuel assets translate to major losses for investors in advanced economies. Nature Climate Change, 12(6), 532-538. https://doi.org/10.1038/s41558-022-01356-y

Starks, L. T. (2023). Presidential address: Sustainable finance and ESG issues—Value versus values. The Journal of Finance, 78(4), 1837-1872. https://doi.org/10.1111/jofi.13255

Chapter 2: Disclosure Regimes, Taxonomies, and Regulatory Infrastructure

If the central failure identified in Chapter 1 is that climate risk goes unpriced because it goes unobserved, the regulatory response follows directly: make firms disclose, define what counts as sustainable, and require supervisors to test the resulting exposures. Over the past decade that response has hardened from voluntary frameworks into binding law across major jurisdictions. This chapter examines the resulting architecture, covering corporate reporting standards, classification systems, prudential supervision, and product labeling rules. It concludes by assessing what this infrastructure can plausibly achieve and where the evidence suggests it changes reporting behavior more than allocation behavior.

The Consolidation of Corporate Sustainability Reporting

Sustainability reporting spent two decades as a voluntary exercise governed by competing frameworks, each with its own metrics and audience. Consolidation has since proceeded along two tracks. The International Sustainability Standards Board has established a global baseline oriented to investor decision-usefulness, while the European Sustainability Reporting Standards impose broader obligations covering impacts on society and the environment as well as financial exposures. Comparable national regimes have followed in a range of jurisdictions, generally aligning with one track or the other.

The substantive divide between them concerns materiality. Financial materiality asks what a reasonable investor needs to know about risks and opportunities affecting enterprise value. Double materiality adds a second test, requiring disclosure of a firm's effects on the environment and society whether or not those effects rebound onto the balance sheet. The distinction is not merely philosophical; it determines the volume of required disclosure, the identity of the intended audience, and the legal exposure attaching to error.

The European architecture illustrates how many separate instruments this now involves. Legislation governs disclosure of company sustainability aspects through the Corporate Sustainability Reporting Directive, the sustainability of economic activities through the Taxonomy Regulation, the sustainability of financial products through the Sustainable Finance Disclosure Regulation, and the environmental, social, and governance risks of credit institutions through Pillar 3 requirements. These mandates are interconnected and have progressed rapidly enough that keeping track of the overall structure has itself become demanding for both researchers and practitioners (Hummel & Jobst, 2024).

The economic case for mandating any of this rests on contested ground. Reviews of the accounting, finance, economics, and management literatures identify plausible capital-market effects, effects on stakeholders other than investors, and effects on firm behavior, but also show that implementation and enforcement design determine whether mandates produce real consequences rather than compliance documents (Christensen et al., 2021). Standardisation reduces the cost of comparison; it does not by itself ensure that anyone acts on what is compared.

Interoperability problems persist despite convergence on a common baseline. Firms operating across jurisdictions must satisfy overlapping requirements whose definitions, boundaries, and assurance expectations do not align precisely, and the residual differences fall disproportionately on the metrics that matter most. Scope 3 emissions illustrate the difficulty: the category covers the majority of reported emissions for most financial and consumer-facing firms, yet it depends on estimates drawn from counterparties whose own reporting may be absent or inconsistent. Aggregating such figures across a portfolio produces a number that is precise in presentation and weakly grounded in measurement.

Assurance is the mechanism intended to close that gap, and it remains immature relative to financial audit. Limited assurance, the prevailing standard in most regimes, tests whether anything has come to the practitioner's attention suggesting misstatement, which is a materially weaker claim than the reasonable assurance applied to financial statements. Until assurance standards and practitioner capacity develop further, sustainability disclosures carry a different evidential status from the financial data they sit alongside, whatever their formal legal standing.

Green Taxonomies and Classification Systems

A taxonomy is a technical screening system that defines when an economic activity qualifies as environmentally sustainable. Its architecture typically combines a substantial contribution test, requiring the activity to advance a stated environmental objective, with a do-no-significant-harm test preventing progress on one objective at the expense of another, alongside minimum social safeguards. The result is a binary determination applied at the level of activities rather than companies.

The EU system is the most developed example and covers activities responsible for up to 80 percent of EU greenhouse gas emissions. Its effectiveness turns almost entirely on the stringency of the technical performance thresholds applied to activities that are not yet green. Analysis of stakeholder responses to a large-scale public consultation indicates that thresholds in several sectors are not calibrated to support the transition toward climate neutrality, and that two distinct use cases should be distinguished: criteria applied to new investment warrant greater stringency than criteria applied to a company's existing activities. Sectors left outside the classification also require differentiation between low-emission activities and those incompatible with a low-carbon future (Schütze & Stede, 2021).

Design choices vary considerably across jurisdictions. Some systems adopt the binary EU approach; others, including several in Asia, use graduated or traffic-light classifications that explicitly accommodate transitional activities rather than excluding them. Graduated systems capture more of the emissions-intensive economy where abatement matters most, at the cost of a weaker signal about what qualifies as genuinely aligned.

Taxonomies matter economically because they define eligible investment universes. Once a classification exists, it propagates into product labeling rules, index construction, bank lending policies, and subsidy eligibility. A threshold set slightly too loosely admits activities that do not belong; set slightly too tightly, it strands activities that need financing precisely because they are not yet clean. Neither error is self-correcting.

The treatment of transitional activities is where this bites hardest. A steel plant replacing blast furnaces with direct reduction technology is doing exactly what decarbonization requires, yet during the transition it remains among the most emissions-intensive assets in any portfolio. Binary classification struggles with this case: the activity is not green by current performance and may never become green by an absolute standard, though financing it delivers more abatement than financing an already-clean activity. Chapter 9 returns to this problem, which no existing classification system has resolved satisfactorily.

A further limitation concerns what taxonomies measure. Alignment is assessed against activity-level technical criteria, not against a company's overall trajectory or the credibility of its plans. A firm can report a rising share of taxonomy-aligned revenue by divesting misaligned businesses to owners with weaker disclosure obligations, improving its reported position while changing nothing about the assets' operation. Activity-level classification is well suited to identifying eligible projects and poorly suited to assessing whether a company is transitioning.

Climate Risk in Prudential Regulation and Supervision

Supervisory attention has moved from whether climate risk is relevant to financial stability toward how it should be measured. The dominant instrument is scenario analysis, in which physical and transition pathways are translated into losses across bank and insurer balance sheets. Central banks and supervisors have adopted common reference scenarios to enable comparison, exploring transition and physical impacts under varying policy ambition over long horizons; short-term variants introduced more recently address near-term financial stability effects, and successive vintages have revised physical damage estimates upward (Network for Greening the Financial System, 2024).

The methodological limits are substantial and increasingly well documented. Climate stress test design would benefit from treating transition risks as dynamic policy choices rather than fixed exogenous paths, incorporating feedback loops between climate and the economy, and examining compound scenarios in which climate risks coincide with other shocks. A structural difficulty is that typical bank loan maturities are short relative to the horizon over which climate risks materialise, which makes it hard to identify channels through which plausible scenarios generate meaningful near-term credit risk. Market-based stress tests using publicly available data offer a complement to supervisory exercises rather than a replacement (Acharya et al., 2023).

The tools themselves vary in quality. Assessment of sixteen climate transition risk analysis tools against criteria drawn from climate science, economics, finance, and risk management found that some perform well across the board, while model transparency, scenario flexibility, treatment of output uncertainty, and communication of assumptions require considerable improvement. Comparable and interpretable risk metrics depend on users understanding and reporting how the underlying tools are configured (Bingler & Senni, 2022).

Scenario analysis also carries an interpretive hazard that its technical presentation obscures. Scenarios are internally consistent explorations of possible futures, not probability-weighted forecasts, yet the outputs are frequently read as loss estimates. When a supervisory exercise reports that a severe transition scenario produces manageable losses, the natural inference is that transition risk is contained. The more defensible inference is that one pathway, under a specific set of modeling assumptions and over a horizon truncated by data availability, produces that result. The gap between those two readings has real consequences for how seriously the findings are taken.

This evidence bears directly on the question of adjusting capital requirements on climate grounds. Prudential capital is calibrated to quantified risk, and the case for a green supporting factor or a brown penalising factor requires confidence in measurement that current tools do not yet support. The alternative view, consistent with the precautionary argument introduced in Chapter 1, holds that waiting for measurement precision guarantees action arrives too late.

Fund Labeling, Anti-Greenwashing Rules, and Product Regulation

Product regulation sits downstream of corporate disclosure and taxonomy design. Disclosure-based regimes require funds to state their sustainability characteristics and then report against them, with naming and marketing rules layered on top to prevent labels from outrunning substance. The intent is that classification constrains behavior.

Evidence that it does so is weak. Analysis of European fund behavior under the Sustainable Finance Disclosure Regulation compared funds declaring sustainability objectives against a control group without them and found that funds self-selecting into opposite categories have incentives to behave similarly on both financial and sustainability dimensions. European funds hardly distinguish sustainability attributes across opposing categories, a pattern described as category fuzziness (Cremasco & Boni, 2022). Disclosure position and portfolio management appear to be only loosely coupled.

A related consequence is that reported market size responds to reclassification rather than to reallocation. When definitions tighten or fund managers reposition products to reduce regulatory exposure, the measured size of the sustainable fund market moves sharply while the underlying holdings barely change. Headline figures on sustainable assets under management therefore track regulatory events as much as investment decisions, and comparisons across periods spanning a regulatory change describe two different measurement conventions rather than a trend.

Enforcement has begun to address the gap between claim and substance, though its reach is limited by what regulators can readily observe. Supervisory action has concentrated on demonstrable misstatements in fund documentation, where a stated exclusion policy conflicts with disclosed holdings, since these are verifiable against public data. Claims about engagement effectiveness, forward-looking alignment, or real-world impact are far harder to falsify and correspondingly harder to police. The predictable response has been a shift in marketing language toward vaguer and less testable formulations, which reduces legal exposure without improving what investors can actually determine about a product.

The theoretical case for mandatory classification is stronger than the empirical record suggests. Modeling private provision of retail ESG funds indicates that greenwashing arises in equilibrium, so a mandatory taxonomy is necessary for sustainable finance to generate real effects. The same analysis, however, finds that a taxonomy improves welfare on top of optimally chosen environmental regulation only where financial frictions constrain socially valuable activity; absent such frictions, environmental policy alone addresses the externality more efficiently (Inderst & Opp, 2024). Classification is a second-best instrument whose value depends on conditions elsewhere in the policy mix.

Regulatory Fragmentation, Compliance Cost, and Market Effects

The cumulative burden of overlapping regimes falls unevenly. Large listed issuers in major jurisdictions can absorb the fixed costs of building reporting infrastructure and spread them across substantial revenue. Smaller issuers and firms in emerging markets face the same requirements without comparable capacity, particularly where obligations reach them indirectly through the supply chains and portfolios of regulated counterparties. The result is a compliance gradient that can restrict access to capital for exactly the firms least equipped to respond.

Early evidence on corporate response is modest. Examination of taxonomy-related disclosures by Austrian nonfinancial companies in the first reporting year, supported by interviews across companies, financial firms, auditors, and non-governmental organisations, found that firms disclosed the required key performance indicators but lacked the reporting infrastructure to provide detailed information. The response is characterized as an endeavour to comply. More encouragingly, interviewees expected lenders to integrate taxonomy data into financing decisions, and implementation triggered internal discussion of strategic positioning and comparison among peer firms (Hummel & Bauernhofer, 2024). Whether that translates into changed capital expenditure remains untested.

This distinction between reporting behavior and allocation behavior is the central question hanging over the entire regulatory edifice. Disclosure mandates reliably produce disclosure. They produce reallocation only where a decision-maker with capital at stake changes what they do in response, and the transmission channel between the two is neither automatic nor well evidenced. The banking channel is the most plausible route, since lenders both consume the information and control credit terms, but the evidence remains largely anticipatory.

Fragmentation carries a second cost that is easy to overlook. Where regimes diverge, firms optimize against whichever framework imposes the least demanding obligation for a given activity, and assets migrate toward owners facing lighter disclosure requirements. Private markets, which fall outside most listed-company reporting mandates, absorb activity that would be more visible on public balance sheets. Aggregate reported emissions across regulated entities can decline while nothing changes in the physical economy, an accounting effect that no individual regime is designed to detect.

What regulatory infrastructure achieves, then, is a precondition rather than an outcome. It makes comparison possible, defines terms that were previously contested, and creates a legal basis for challenging false claims. None of that changes the relative returns on low-carbon and emissions-intensive assets, which is the variable that governs where capital goes. The instruments that act on returns directly are the subject of the chapters that follow.

References

Acharya, V. V., Berner, R., Engle, R. F., Jung, H., Stroebel, J., Zeng, X., & Zhao, Y. (2023). Climate stress testing. Annual Review of Financial Economics, 15(1), 291-326. https://doi.org/10.1146/annurev-financial-110921-101555

Bingler, J., & Senni, C. C. (2022). Taming the green swan: a criteria-based analysis to improve the understanding of climate-related financial risk assessment tools. Climate Policy, 22(3), 356-370. https://doi.org/10.1080/14693062.2022.2032569

Christensen, H. B., Hail, L., & Leuz, C. (2021). Mandatory CSR and sustainability reporting: economic analysis and literature review. Review of Accounting Studies, 26(3), 1176-1248. https://doi.org/10.1007/s11142-021-09609-5

Cremasco, C., & Boni, L. (2022). Is the European Union (EU) Sustainable Finance Disclosure Regulation (SFDR) effective in shaping sustainability objectives? An analysis of investment funds' behaviour. Journal of Sustainable Finance & Investment, 14(4), 1018-1036. https://doi.org/10.1080/20430795.2022.2124838

Hummel, K., & Bauernhofer, K. (2024). Consequences of sustainability reporting mandates: evidence from the EU taxonomy regulation. Accounting Forum, 48(3), 374-400. https://doi.org/10.1080/01559982.2024.2301854

Hummel, K., & Jobst, D. (2024). An overview of corporate sustainability reporting legislation in the European Union. Accounting in Europe, 21(3), 320-355. https://doi.org/10.1080/17449480.2024.2312145

Inderst, R., & Opp, M. M. (2024). Sustainable finance versus environmental policy: Does greenwashing justify a taxonomy for sustainable investments? Journal of Financial Economics, 163, 103954. https://doi.org/10.1016/j.jfineco.2024.103954

Network for Greening the Financial System. (2024). NGFS Climate Scenarios for Central Banks and Supervisors. Network for Greening the Financial System. https://www.ngfs.net/en/publications-and-statistics/publications/ngfs-climate-scenarios-central-banks-and-supervisors

Schütze, F., & Stede, J. (2021). The EU sustainable finance taxonomy and its contribution to climate neutrality. Journal of Sustainable Finance & Investment, 14(1), 128-160. https://doi.org/10.1080/20430795.2021.2006129

Chapter 3: ESG Integration in Investment Analysis and Portfolio Construction

The disclosure architecture examined in Chapter 2 exists to supply investors with information. This chapter examines what happens to that information once it reaches them. It covers the data infrastructure underpinning ESG analysis, the well-documented divergence among rating providers, the techniques by which sustainability factors enter security selection and portfolio construction, and the evidence on whether any of it changes financial or environmental outcomes. Stewardship and engagement are treated as a separate transmission channel from portfolio exclusion, since the two operate through different mechanisms and carry different evidence.

ESG Data Infrastructure and Its Structural Limitations

ESG analysis rests on three types of input: figures reported by companies, figures estimated by data vendors where reporting is absent, and alternative data drawn from sources such as satellite imagery, regulatory filings, and media monitoring. The proportions matter. Where reported data is thin, vendor estimation models fill the gap, and the resulting scores describe modeled expectations for a firm of that size, sector, and geography as much as they describe the firm itself.

Coverage bias follows predictably from this structure. Large listed companies in jurisdictions with mandatory reporting generate abundant data. Smaller issuers, private companies, and firms in emerging markets generate less, and estimation substitutes accordingly. Because estimation models are typically anchored on sector and regional averages, they compress genuine variation: a small emerging-market firm with strong practices and one with weak practices converge toward the same modeled score. Analysis built on such data systematically understates the dispersion it is meant to detect.

A subtler problem concerns what the data measures. Many widely used indicators capture the existence of policies, committees, and disclosures rather than outcomes. A company scores well for having an environmental management system, publishing a target, and reporting emissions, none of which establishes that its emissions are falling. Disclosure quality and environmental performance are distinct properties, and metrics that conflate them reward transparency over substance. This creates a mechanical advantage for firms with the resources to report thoroughly, which is not the same as an advantage for firms doing better.

Timing introduces a further distortion. Sustainability data arrives annually, often with a lag of six to twelve months between the reporting period and vendor publication, while security prices adjust continuously. An analyst acting on an ESG score is therefore acting on a description of the firm as it was more than a year earlier. For slow-moving structural characteristics such as asset composition this matters little; for controversies, management changes, or capital expenditure decisions it matters a great deal, and these are precisely the developments most likely to be financially material.

These limitations propagate downstream. Every rating, index, benchmark, and regulatory alignment calculation is built on this foundation, and the confidence attached to outputs frequently exceeds what the inputs support. The problem is not that the data is useless but that its precision is routinely overstated. Scores are reported to decimal places and used to rank issuers within narrow bands, when the underlying measurement supports little more than a coarse sorting into broad categories.

Rating Divergence and Measurement Disagreement

The most thoroughly documented feature of ESG data is that providers disagree. Examination of ratings from six prominent agencies, mapping their methodologies onto a common taxonomy of categories, decomposes the divergence into three components. Measurement contributes 56 percent, scope 38 percent, and weighting 6 percent. Further analysis identifies a rater effect, in which an agency's overall view of a firm influences how it measures specific categories, suggesting that assessments are not formed independently across dimensions (Berg et al., 2022).

The decomposition is analytically important because the components have different implications. Weighting disagreement is legitimate and irreducible, reflecting genuine differences in judgment about how much governance should count relative to emissions. Scope disagreement reflects different views about which issues belong in an assessment. Measurement disagreement is more troubling, since it means providers observing the same construct with the same intent produce different readings of it. That measurement dominates the decomposition points to the data layer rather than to methodology as the primary source of confusion.

The consequences reach beyond the ratings themselves. Analysis of agency criteria shows a lack of commonality in defining ESG characteristics, attributes, and standards, with agreement across providers substantially low and agencies reaching opposite conclusions about the same companies. Because alternative definitions generate different investment universes, they generate different benchmarks, and manager skill becomes difficult to assess when performance is strongly conditioned by the chosen benchmark. Score disagreement also disperses the effect of ESG investor preferences on asset prices, weakening the very price signal that integration is supposed to transmit (Billio et al., 2021).

This last point deserves emphasis. If sustainable investing is expected to raise the cost of capital for poor performers, that mechanism requires investors to agree about who the poor performers are. Persistent disagreement fragments the pressure across inconsistent targets and dilutes it everywhere.

Whether convergence is achievable is genuinely contested. One view holds that divergence is a transitional feature of an immature data industry, and that mandatory disclosure of standardized metrics will narrow it as estimation gives way to reporting. The competing view holds that divergence is intrinsic, because ESG is not a single latent quality awaiting accurate measurement but a bundle of loosely related attributes that reasonable analysts weight differently according to their purpose. The decomposition evidence favours the first view for the measurement component and the second for scope and weighting. Standardized disclosure should reduce measurement disagreement without touching the question of which issues belong in an assessment or how much each should count.

There is also a case that aggregate scores are the wrong unit of analysis. A single composite combining emissions intensity, labour practices, and board independence answers no specific investment question, and its usefulness declines as its breadth increases. Investors seeking to assess transition risk need emissions and capital expenditure data, not a blended score in which those figures are diluted by unrelated governance indicators. The practical response among sophisticated users has been to bypass composites in favour of underlying raw metrics, which sidesteps weighting disagreement while leaving measurement problems intact.

Integration Techniques in Security Selection and Valuation

ESG factors enter investment analysis through several distinct methods that are frequently discussed as though interchangeable. Exclusionary screening removes securities or sectors from the investable universe on normative or risk grounds. Norms-based screening excludes issuers violating international conventions. Best-in-class tilting overweights higher-scoring issuers within each sector, preserving sector exposure while shifting composition. Thematic allocation directs capital toward defined activities such as clean energy or water. Fundamental integration adjusts cash flow projections or discount rates to reflect sustainability-related risks within an otherwise conventional valuation.

The methods also differ in what they assume about market efficiency. Fundamental integration is a claim that sustainability information is not yet fully reflected in prices, and that an analyst who incorporates it will value securities more accurately than the market does. This is an active management proposition, and it implies the advantage erodes as the information becomes widely used. Screening makes no such claim: it operates on eligibility regardless of whether the excluded securities are correctly priced. Conflating the two produces the common but incoherent position that ESG integration both generates persistent excess returns and reflects information already priced by everyone.

Only the last of these is integration in a strict sense. The others operate on the universe or its weights, leaving the valuation of individual securities untouched. The distinction matters because a screen applied after an investment case has been formed does not change the analyst's view of value; it changes only whether the position is permitted. Much of what is described as ESG integration in practice is screening with a different label.

Each method carries structural consequences for portfolio risk. Exclusions introduce tracking error against conventional benchmarks and shift factor exposures, often unintentionally: removing energy and materials tilts a portfolio toward growth and quality characteristics and away from value. Best-in-class tilting constrains those distortions but dilutes the signal, since a high-scoring issuer in an emissions-intensive sector may still have a larger absolute footprint than a low-scoring issuer in a services sector.

Asset pricing theory clarifies what these techniques should be expected to do. A model with partial segmentation and heterogeneous preferences distinguishes an exclusion premium, generalising the classical premium on neglected stocks, from a taste premium reflecting investor preferences. Applied to US equities, the average annual exclusion effect for sin stocks is 2.79 percent over 1999 to 2019, while the annual taste effect ranges from negative 1.12 percent to positive 0.14 percent across industries for 2007 to 2019, with a within-industry spread between top and bottom terciles that can exceed 2 percent per year (Zerbib, 2022). Exclusion, in other words, raises expected returns on excluded assets, which is the mirror image of raising their cost of capital.

Portfolio Construction, Decarbonization Targets, and Benchmark Design

At portfolio level, ESG considerations are increasingly expressed as quantified decarbonization trajectories rather than as scores. Climate-aligned benchmarks impose a starting reduction in carbon intensity relative to a parent index followed by a fixed annual decline. Net-zero alignment frameworks add forward-looking measures assessing whether holdings have credible transition plans.

The central analytical issue is that portfolio carbon intensity can be reduced without any change in real-economy emissions. Selling shares in an emissions-intensive company transfers ownership to another investor; the plant continues to operate. Reported financed emissions fall for the seller and rise for the buyer, and the aggregate is unchanged. A portfolio can therefore meet a decarbonization trajectory through reweighting alone, and a fund reporting steady annual intensity reductions may have financed no abatement whatsoever.

The composition of capital allocation compounds this. Analysis of ESG transmission mechanisms through ratings, engagement, and capital allocation finds that broad ESG indices, which do not meaningfully facilitate sustainability, dominate current investing, while the darker green indices that could plausibly have impact hold far less capital. The resulting mismatch between labeled volume and allocative effect is described as the ESG capital allocation gap, and it turns on the standard-setting role of a small number of index providers whose methodological choices determine where enormous pools of passive capital settle (Fichtner et al., 2023).

Forward-looking alignment metrics were designed to address exactly this weakness by assessing trajectory rather than current footprint.

Their difficulty is evidentiary. Assessing whether a transition plan is credible requires judgment about technology costs, policy durability, and management intent over decades, and the resulting scores carry far wider uncertainty than the emissions data they are meant to supplement. Two analysts assessing the same plan can reasonably reach opposite conclusions, which reintroduces at the portfolio level the divergence problem documented for ratings.

Constraint stacking introduces a further cost. Each additional requirement, whether an exclusion list, an intensity target, or a minimum rating threshold, narrows the feasible set. Individually modest constraints combine to produce concentrated portfolios with meaningful unintended factor exposures, and the resulting risk is borne for a benefit that, as the divestment analysis above suggests, may be largely notional.

Stewardship, Engagement, and the Evidence on Performance

Engagement offers a different transmission channel. Rather than adjusting exposure, investors use ownership rights to influence corporate behavior through dialogue, proxy voting, shareholder resolutions, and escalation. The logic is straightforward: a retained holding preserves the standing to exert influence that divestment forfeits.

Evidence on engagement is more encouraging than evidence on exclusion. Analysis of ESG engagement outcomes finds that it reduces firms' downside risk, measured through value at risk and lower partial moments, with the value at risk of engagement targets falling by 9 percent of the standard deviation following successful engagements relative to control firms. Effects are strongest for environmental topics, primarily climate change, and targets showing large downside risk reductions exhibit a subsequent decrease in environmental incidents, which links the financial result to an observable change in conduct (Hoepner et al., 2023).

Engagement carries structural limits alongside its advantages. It depends on ownership, so it reaches listed companies and has little purchase on private firms, state-owned enterprises, or the privately held assets that increasingly absorb emissions-intensive activity. It also faces a collective action problem: the costs of engagement fall on the engaging investor while the benefits accrue to all holders, which explains why coordination through investor coalitions has become the dominant model and why free-riding remains endemic.

Success is conditional rather than automatic. Study of 553 collaborative climate engagements coordinated through the Principles for Responsible Investment shows that coalition size, shareholding stake, experience, and local access combine into four distinct configurations tailored to target firms' financial capacity and environmental receptivity. Unsuccessful engagements emphasize single levers at the expense of others, and the mechanisms underlying effective coalitions involve synchronising activity, contextualising demands, and avoiding excessive narrowness of focus (Slager et al., 2023). Engagement is a capability requiring resources and design, not a costless alternative to divestment.

The broader empirical literature on ESG and financial performance should be read with the measurement problems described earlier firmly in view. Studies relating ESG scores to returns inherit the divergence documented across providers, so results depend materially on which rating is used, and the distinction between risk mitigation and return generation is frequently blurred. The defensible conclusions are narrow: engagement on environmental issues reduces measurable downside risk; exclusion raises expected returns on excluded assets while transferring rather than eliminating exposure; and the aggregate effect of ESG integration on real-economy emissions remains weakly evidenced. Claims that outrun these findings are common, and Chapter 5 examines what a stronger claim about outcomes would actually require.

References

Berg, F., Kölbel, J. F., & Rigobón, R. (2022). Aggregate confusion: The divergence of ESG ratings. European Finance Review, 26(6), 1315-1344. https://doi.org/10.1093/rof/rfac033

Billio, M., Costola, M., Hristova, I., Latino, C., & Pelizzon, L. (2021). Inside the ESG ratings: (Dis)agreement and performance. Corporate Social Responsibility and Environmental Management, 28(5), 1426-1445. https://doi.org/10.1002/csr.2177

Fichtner, J., Jaspert, R., & Petry, J. (2023). Mind the ESG capital allocation gap: The role of index providers, standard-setting, and "green" indices for the creation of sustainability impact. Regulation & Governance, 18(2), 479-498. https://doi.org/10.1111/rego.12530

Hoepner, A. G. F., Oikonomou, I., Sautner, Z., Starks, L. T., & Zhou, X. Y. (2023). ESG shareholder engagement and downside risk. European Finance Review, 28(2), 483-510. https://doi.org/10.1093/rof/rfad034

Slager, R., Chuah, K., Gond, J. P., Furnari, S., & Homanen, M. (2023). Tailor-to-target: Configuring collaborative shareholder engagements on climate change. Management Science, 69(12), 7693-7718. https://doi.org/10.1287/mnsc.2023.4806

Zerbib, O. (2022). A sustainable capital asset pricing model (S-CAPM): Evidence from environmental integration and sin stock exclusion. European Finance Review, 26(6), 1345-1388. https://doi.org/10.1093/rof/rfac045

Chapter 4: Green, Social, and Sustainability-Linked Debt Markets

Labeled debt is where sustainable finance has achieved its greatest volume, and it is the segment most often cited as evidence that capital markets have engaged seriously with the transition. This chapter examines how these instruments actually function. It distinguishes use-of-proceeds structures from performance-linked structures as two separate financing logics, assesses the verification infrastructure supporting both, examines the contested question of whether labeling reduces borrowing costs, and considers sovereign issuance and the specific weaknesses that have emerged in performance-linked design.

Use-of-Proceeds Instruments and Market Standards

The dominant structure in labeled debt is the use-of-proceeds bond. An issuer raises capital under a framework specifying eligible project categories, allocates the proceeds to qualifying expenditures, tracks the allocation, and reports on it periodically alongside indicators of environmental or social outcomes. Green bonds finance environmental projects, social bonds finance projects with social objectives, and sustainability bonds combine both. Voluntary market principles supply the template, and taxonomy-based regulation increasingly supplies the eligibility criteria.

The market has reached considerable scale. Green issuance dominates the labeled market, accounting for 68 percent of cumulative emerging market issuance and 65 percent in advanced markets (World Bank Treasury, 2025). Growth on this trajectory has established labeled debt as a routine funding instrument rather than a specialist product.

The structural feature that most often goes unremarked is that a use-of-proceeds label does not alter the credit risk of the instrument. Bondholders have recourse to the issuer's whole balance sheet, not to the specific projects financed. A green bond issued by a diversified energy company ranks equally with that company's conventional debt, carries the same default probability, and would recover identically in insolvency. The label describes an accounting relationship between the proceeds and a set of expenditures; it does not create a ring-fenced claim.

This has a direct implication for additionality. Because capital is fungible, an issuer with an existing pipeline of eligible projects can label a bond against expenditures it would have made anyway, then use the freed-up conventional funding capacity for other purposes. The resulting instrument satisfies every requirement of the framework while financing nothing that would not otherwise have occurred. Whether labeling changes real investment therefore cannot be inferred from issuance volumes, which is the metric most frequently used to demonstrate the market's significance.

Impact reporting is the mechanism intended to demonstrate that something was achieved, and its quality varies widely. Issuers report indicators such as installed renewable capacity, avoided emissions, or beneficiaries served, typically calculated using their own methodologies against baselines they select. Avoided emissions figures are particularly sensitive to baseline choice, since the same solar installation generates very different avoided-emissions claims depending on whether it is compared against the average grid emissions factor or the marginal generator it actually displaces. Aggregating such figures across a portfolio of bonds produces totals whose components were computed on incompatible assumptions.

The evidence on real effects is mixed but not empty. Analysis of how green bond issuance affects corporate environmental outcomes finds that issuance significantly improves firms' overall environmental performance and their capacity to develop new environmental technologies and processes, while the effect on carbon emissions intensity is less clear and requires one or more additional years to appear (Benlemlih et al., 2022). Issuance appears to accompany genuine operational change, with a lag, though the direction of causation between committed firms and the instruments they select is difficult to isolate.

Sustainability-Linked Instruments and Performance Conditionality

Sustainability-linked bonds and loans invert the logic. Proceeds are unrestricted and available for general corporate purposes, while the coupon adjusts according to whether the issuer meets predefined sustainability performance targets measured against key performance indicators. The instrument finances the company rather than a project, which makes it available to issuers whose transition requires changing existing operations rather than building new assets. That is precisely the population that use-of-proceeds structures serve poorly.

The design depends entirely on calibration. Potential to promote transition rests on a common understanding of eligible activities and material performance indicators, on science-based targets as best practice, on issuers dispelling greenwashing concerns, and on bond characteristics that create meaningful incentives to improve carbon performance (Vulturius et al., 2022). Each of these conditions has proved difficult to satisfy in practice.

Pricing evidence indicates where calibration has failed. Examination of sustainability-linked bond pricing finds investors accept a yield 1 to 2 basis points lower for the ESG label, and that the average probability of missing the target is 14 to 39 percent, indicating that firms set targets that are easy to reach. The market itself prices these instruments efficiently: prices depend strongly on the size of the potential penalty, with no evidence of mispricing, and the instruments function partly as financial hedges against ESG risk (Feldhütter et al., 2024).

That combination is analytically damning for the instrument's stated purpose. If targets are set at levels the issuer expects to meet, the contingent penalty is unlikely to be triggered, and a penalty unlikely to be triggered exerts little influence on behavior. The market is not mispricing these bonds; it is pricing them correctly as instruments with weak conditionality. Common design weaknesses reinforce this: observation dates set close to or after maturity, step-ups too small relative to funding costs to alter investment decisions, and indicators measuring intensity rather than absolute emissions, which permits reported improvement alongside rising output. Issuance in this segment has contracted after early rapid growth, which is consistent with issuers concluding that reputational scrutiny outweighs the modest pricing benefit.

Verification, Second-Party Opinions, and Assurance

Neither structure is self-certifying, so an external review industry has developed around both. Second-party opinions assess whether a framework aligns with market principles before issuance. Verification and certification schemes test alignment against defined standards. Post-issuance assurance examines whether proceeds were allocated as stated.

The commercial dynamics of this market create familiar problems. Reviews are commissioned and paid for by issuers, who select the provider and have an evident interest in a favorable opinion. Providers compete on price and turnaround alongside rigor. The resulting incentive structure resembles that of credit rating agencies, with the difference that no comparable regulatory framework governs conflicts or methodology disclosure in most jurisdictions.

The scope of most reviews is also narrower than their reception suggests. A second-party opinion typically assesses whether a framework is consistent with stated principles, not whether the projects it describes will deliver environmental benefit, whether they are additional, or whether the issuer's broader strategy is aligned with anything. An opinion confirming that a framework meets the Green Bond Principles establishes procedural conformity. It is frequently read as a substantive endorsement of environmental merit, which it does not provide and does not claim to.

Post-issuance assurance is weaker still, and is frequently omitted entirely. Where it occurs, it generally confirms that an amount equal to the proceeds was allocated to categories described in the framework. It does not test whether the expenditure was incremental, whether the projects performed as projected, or whether the reported impact figures are defensible. The distinction between confirming that money was spent on eligible things and confirming that the spending achieved something is the distinction between the assurance that exists and the assurance the market's rhetoric implies.

Regulated labels and emerging standards change these obligations by making verification a supervised activity with defined content, registration requirements for providers, and mandatory pre- and post-issuance review. This addresses the conflict-of-interest problem partially, by imposing professional standards, while leaving the fundamental issuer-pays structure intact.

Pricing Effects and the Greenium Debate

Whether labeled debt prices at a premium to comparable conventional debt has attracted more empirical attention than any other question in this market, and the answers depend heavily on methodology. The measurement problem is constructing a counterfactual: green bonds differ from conventional bonds in issuer, currency, maturity, size, and rating, so any raw yield comparison confounds the label with these characteristics.

Careful matching finds a measurable effect. Analysis using roughly 2,000 green and 180,000 non-green bonds from 650 international issuers, applying propensity score matching and coarsened exact matching to construct comparable samples, finds green bond yields 15 to 20 basis points lower than conventional bonds in both primary and secondary markets. The same analysis notes that green bonds have larger issue sizes and lower rated issuers on average, which is why matching is necessary rather than optional (Löffler et al., 2021).

The interpretation of a premium of this size requires care. Fifteen to twenty basis points is a genuine funding advantage, particularly for frequent issuers, but it is small relative to the capital expenditure it supports. On a ten-year bond, a 20 basis point saving reduces financing costs by roughly 2 percent of principal over the instrument's life, which does not turn an uneconomic project into an economic one. The pricing advantage is better understood as a modest reward for a costly signal than as a mechanism capable of redirecting investment at scale.

Issuer characteristics complicate the picture further. Companies choosing to issue labeled debt differ systematically from those that do not, tending to be larger, more frequently rated, more exposed to public scrutiny, and more advanced in sustainability reporting. Any of these attributes could independently support tighter pricing. Matching techniques control for observable differences but cannot control for the unobservable qualities that led a firm to issue a labeled instrument in the first place, which means part of the measured premium plausibly reflects issuer selection rather than the label itself.

Several drivers of the premium are also unrelated to environmental merit. Scarcity relative to mandated demand, index inclusion, and investor mandates requiring labeled holdings all support pricing independently of what the proceeds finance. Where those mandates bind, the premium reflects a supply constraint. As issuance grows and the constraint relaxes, the premium should compress, which is what would be expected of a market clearing rather than of a durable environmental repricing.

Sovereign Issuance and Market Development in Emerging Economies

Sovereign labeled issuance serves purposes beyond funding. Governments issuing green or sustainability bonds establish a pricing benchmark for domestic corporate issuers, signal policy commitment to international investors, and impose internal discipline by requiring budget expenditures to be classified and reported against environmental criteria.

Evidence from developing-country issuance clarifies both the motivations and the limits. Analysis of sovereign climate-aligned bonds, drawing on interviews with issuance managers and expert organisations and examining Seychelles' blue bond and Indonesia's green sukuk, finds that gaps in public budgets were the main domestic trigger for issuance, with international organisations including the World Bank and UNDP exercising influence. Perceived benefits of capital mobilization, new investor access, and transparency were judged to outweigh additionality concerns and reputational risk, though higher transaction costs relative to conventional issuance remained a consideration. The same analysis finds that risk-return rationales and the exclusion of climate from country risk profiling place developing countries in a more challenging position, and that a legacy of exclusionary dynamics in private markets remains a structural barrier (Chavarría-Flores & Warren, 2024).

Emerging-market sovereign issuance faces constraints that labeling does not touch. Currency risk dominates: a sovereign issuing in hard currency to finance domestic-currency revenue-generating assets accepts a mismatch that can overwhelm any environmental benefit if the exchange rate moves. Issuing in local currency avoids the mismatch but narrows the investor base sharply. Credit ratings impose a second constraint, since many institutional mandates prohibit sub-investment-grade holdings regardless of instrument label, which excludes most of the countries where the investment gap is largest. Project pipeline capacity imposes a third, as labeled issuance requires a stock of identified, classified, and reportable expenditures that many finance ministries have not yet assembled.

The finding that budget gaps drove issuance is worth dwelling on. It indicates that sovereign labeled bonds functioned primarily as a financing response to fiscal pressure, with the environmental label serving to widen the investor base rather than to reorient expenditure. This is not illegitimate, but it locates the instrument's value in market access rather than in changed public investment.

What labeled debt markets have changed is the visibility and classification of capital, the investor base available to issuers willing to report, and, at the margin, funding costs. What they have not changed is the fundamental economics of the underlying assets. A project that does not clear its cost of capital conventionally does not clear it because the bond financing it carries a label, and the small pricing benefits documented here are not large enough to close that gap. The instruments that attempt to close it directly are the subject of the next two chapters.

References

Benlemlih, M., Jaballah, J., & Kermiche, L. (2022). Does financing strategy accelerate corporate energy transition? Evidence from green bonds. Business Strategy and the Environment, 32(1), 878-889. https://doi.org/10.1002/bse.3180

Chavarría-Flores, A., & Warren, P. (2024). Sovereign climate bonds: Policy innovation for just transitions in developing countries. Journal of Climate Finance, 7, 100041. https://doi.org/10.1016/j.jclimf.2024.100041

Feldhütter, P., Halskov, K., & Krebbers, A. (2024). Pricing of sustainability-linked bonds. Journal of Financial Economics, 162, 103944. https://doi.org/10.1016/j.jfineco.2024.103944

Löffler, K. U., Petreski, A., & Stephan, A. (2021). Drivers of green bond issuance and new evidence on the "greenium". Eurasian Economic Review, 11(1), 1-24. https://doi.org/10.1007/s40822-020-00165-y

Vulturius, G., Maltais, A., & Forsbacka, K. (2022). Sustainability-linked bonds – their potential to promote issuers' transition to net-zero emissions and future research directions. Journal of Sustainable Finance & Investment, 14(1), 116-127. https://doi.org/10.1080/20430795.2022.2040943

World Bank Treasury. (2025). Labeled Sustainable Bonds Market Update, June 2025. World Bank Treasury. https://thedocs.worldbank.org/en/doc/c7d5bdd94c82fb169fbdff12d46fe319-0340012025/original/Labeled-Bond-Quarterly-Newsletter-Issue-No-11.pdf

Chapter 5: Impact Investing and the Measurement of Outcomes

Impact investing makes a stronger claim than any mechanism examined so far. Where ESG integration asserts that sustainability factors are financially material, and labeled debt asserts that proceeds were allocated to eligible categories, impact investing asserts causation: that the investment produced an outcome which would not otherwise have occurred. This chapter examines what that claim requires, the frameworks built to substantiate it, the return expectations that segment the market, and the persistent difficulty of verifying a counterfactual. The gap between what is claimed and what can be demonstrated defines the field's central problem.

Intentionality, Additionality, and the Definition of Impact

Three criteria conventionally distinguish impact investment from conventional or ESG-screened investment. Intentionality requires that positive social or environmental outcomes be a deliberate objective rather than an incidental byproduct. Contribution requires that the investor add something the outcome would not have had otherwise. Measurement requires that the outcome be specified in advance and assessed against evidence. All three are necessary; intentionality alone is a statement of purpose that any investor can make costlessly.

Contribution is where the analytical weight sits, and it divides into two distinct concepts routinely conflated in practice. Enterprise additionality asks whether the investee organization produces outcomes that would not have occurred without it, which is a question about the business. Investor additionality asks whether the investor's participation changed what the enterprise was able to do, which is a question about the capital. An investor can hold shares in a genuinely impactful company while adding nothing at all, if the company would have raised the same capital on the same terms from someone else.

Secondary market transactions expose this distinction sharply. Purchasing listed equity in a renewable energy developer transfers ownership from one holder to another. The company receives no new capital, its investment program is unchanged, and the transaction's effect on real outcomes operates only through the marginal influence of that trade on the share price and thus on the firm's future cost of capital. That channel exists but is small, and describing such a purchase as an impact investment stretches the contribution criterion past the point where it does any work.

Contribution can also take non-financial forms that the capital-focused framing understates. An investor supplying governance expertise, market access, or technical assistance alongside capital may change what an enterprise achieves even where the funding itself was replaceable. These contributions are real, but they are harder to evidence than a financing gap and correspondingly easier to assert without support, which is why frameworks that recognize them also tend to require documentation of the specific mechanism claimed.

Private market investment in capital-constrained enterprises presents a much stronger case, since capital is provided directly to an organization whose activities expand as a result. This is why credible impact claims cluster in private debt, private equity, and real assets, and why the migration of the impact label into listed products has diluted its meaning. The label has grown considerably faster than the set of transactions that can support the underlying claim.

Impact Measurement and Management Frameworks

A substantial infrastructure has developed to specify, measure, and report impact. Dimensional frameworks disaggregate impact into what outcome occurs, who experiences it, how much occurs, the contribution made relative to what would have happened anyway, and the risk that the expected impact does not materialise. Standardized metric catalogues supply comparable indicators across sectors. Operating principles specify how impact considerations should be embedded across the investment lifecycle, from origination through exit, with independent verification of the management system.

These frameworks share a structural tension between comparability and relevance. Standardized metrics allow aggregation across a portfolio and comparison between managers, which is what allocators require. Yet the metrics that genuinely capture whether an intervention worked are usually specific to that intervention, and forcing them into common categories discards the information that mattered. Reporting that a portfolio reached a given number of beneficiaries aggregates cleanly and says almost nothing about whether any of them are better off.

Verification practice compounds the difficulty. Independent assurance in impact investing typically examines whether the manager has an impact management system and follows it, which is a process audit rather than an outcome audit. Confirming that a manager applies its stated methodology consistently establishes nothing about whether the methodology measures anything real. The distinction parallels the one drawn in Chapter 4 between procedural conformity and substantive merit, and it recurs wherever verification is commissioned by the party being verified.

Impact risk is the dimension most often omitted in practice, and its omission is revealing. Reporting conventions treat achieved outcomes as certain once measured, when in fact every impact estimate carries uncertainty from measurement error, attribution assumptions, and the possibility that effects decay after the reporting period. Financial reporting has developed extensive conventions for expressing uncertainty, including ranges, sensitivities, and provisions. Impact reporting has largely not, and the resulting figures are presented with a confidence that their derivation does not support.

The market these frameworks serve is now substantial. Estimates constructed from a database of direct impact assets under management, cleared of duplicates and indirect investments, put the market at USD 1.571 trillion across more than 3,900 organisations, growing at 21 percent annually since 2019, with pension funds, insurance companies, and other institutional investors now among its major participants (Global Impact Investing Network, 2024). Institutional participation on this scale raises the stakes attached to measurement quality considerably.

Return Expectations, Concessionality, and Capital Segmentation

Impact capital divides into two segments with different economics. Market-rate impact investors seek returns comparable to conventional investments in the same asset class and risk profile, on the view that impact and financial return are compatible in well-chosen opportunities. Concessionary investors accept below-market returns deliberately, treating the shortfall as the price of an outcome the market will not fund.

The distinction determines which objectives can attract private capital at all. Where an activity generates contractible revenue, market-rate capital is available and the constraint is deal flow. Where the benefit is a public good with no revenue stream attached, no amount of investor enthusiasm substitutes for a payer, and only concessionary or public capital will fund it. Much confusion in the field stems from proposing market-rate solutions to problems whose defining feature is the absence of a revenue model.

Asset class matters more than the market-rate debate usually acknowledges. Renewable energy infrastructure in stable jurisdictions offers contracted, inflation-linked cash flows that institutional investors value on their financial merits alone, and describing such investments as concessionary would be inaccurate. Early-stage enterprises serving low-income populations present the opposite profile, with high failure rates, long horizons, and small

absolute returns. Aggregating both into a single statement about impact investment returns produces a number that describes neither.

Evidence on realized returns is complicated by selection effects that are difficult to correct. Reported performance is drawn from managers choosing to report, in vintages that have completed their cycle, using valuations that are frequently self-assessed for illiquid holdings. Funds that performed poorly are less likely to appear in the sample. These problems afflict private markets generally, but they bear more heavily on impact investing because the claim being tested is that no return sacrifice is required, and survivorship bias points in exactly the direction that would produce that finding spuriously.

Investor behavior itself provides an unexpectedly direct test of how impact is valued. A framed field experiment assessing willingness to pay for sustainable investments found that investors display substantial willingness to pay for sustainability but do not pay significantly more for greater impact, a result that holds even among dedicated impact investors. Willingness to pay responds to relative rather than absolute impact levels when several investments are compared, and investors report positive emotions when choosing sustainable investments regardless of the magnitude of impact achieved. The valuation of impact appears emotional rather than calculative (Heeb et al., 2022).

That finding has uncomfortable implications. If capital does not price impact magnitude, then competition among impact investments will not systematically direct capital toward the most effective interventions, and managers face no market discipline to maximize outcomes rather than to document them attractively.

Outcome-Based Instruments and Results-Linked Finance

Outcome-based instruments attempt to solve the measurement problem contractually by making payment conditional on verified

results. Impact bonds involve investors financing delivery upfront, a service provider implementing an intervention, and an outcome payer repaying investors with a return only if agreed outcomes are independently verified. Results-based financing and outcome funds apply similar logic in development and public service contexts.

The evidence base is thinner and more mixed than the model's elegance suggests. A scoping review of social impact bonds financing non-communicable disease prevention, drawing on published and grey literature across eight databases, identified eleven instruments implemented in eight countries from 83 eligible studies, and found that only three met all their target outcomes. Instruments that succeeded shared evidence-based interventions, multiple service providers, and an intermediated structure. Conflict of interest and absence of public disclosure were common across the literature, and the average private initial investment was approximately USD 2.0 million (Hulse et al., 2021). At that scale, transaction and verification costs consume a substantial share of the capital deployed.

Transaction costs explain much of the limited uptake. Structuring an outcome contract requires agreeing measurable indicators, an attribution methodology, a verification process, and a payment schedule among parties whose interests diverge on every one of those points. The negotiation is expensive relative to deal size, and the resulting complexity restricts participation to well-resourced intermediaries. Attribution presents the deepest obstacle: outcomes in health, education, and employment depend on many factors beyond any single intervention, and constructing a payment trigger that isolates the provider's contribution is genuinely difficult rather than merely administratively burdensome.

Governance consequences also follow from the contractual structure. A longitudinal qualitative study of a major UK social impact bond addressing social determinants of health examined whether outcomes-based contracting moves public services toward New Public Governance or back toward New Public Management. Both logics were present at initiation, but managerial elements strengthened over time while collaborative elements weakened, driven by two features inseparable from the model: investor power and the data requirements of contract management. The instrument promoted retrenchment of New Public Management rather than hybridisation (French et al., 2022).

This is a significant finding for a mechanism promoted partly on the grounds that it enables innovation and flexibility in service delivery. The measurement apparatus required to make payment contingent on outcomes generates precisely the standardisation and control that outcome contracting was meant to escape. The instrument's defining strength and its principal limitation have the same source.

Impact Washing, Attribution, and the Limits of Verification

Weak measurement standards permit claims that do not withstand scrutiny, and the reputational consequences have begun to arrive. The pattern resembles that documented for ESG products in Chapter 3: as the label attracts capital, products adopt it with progressively weaker justification, and the average substance behind the claim declines even as the aggregate reported figure grows.

The root difficulty is the counterfactual. Establishing impact requires knowing what would have happened absent the investment, which is unobservable by construction. Rigorous evaluation methods exist, including randomised designs and quasi-experimental approaches, but they are expensive, slow, and frequently infeasible for a single financing transaction. Most impact reporting substitutes attribution by assertion: outputs are counted, associated with the investment, and reported as impact without any counterfactual having been constructed.

Theoretical work on the principal alternative to direct financing sharpens the point considerably. Modeling the cost of capital effect of divestiture as a function of the socially conscious capital share, the fraction of targeted firms, and the return correlation between targeted and other firms shows that the calibrated effect is too small to meaningfully affect real investment decisions. Empirical examination of firms changing ESG status detects no effect on their cost of capital, and the conclusion drawn is that socially conscious investors should invest and exercise control rights rather than divest (Berk & van Binsbergen, 2024).

A complementary model reaches a compatible conclusion by a different route. Green investing raises the cost of capital of carbon-intensive companies and induces emissions reductions that increase with the wealth share of green investors and their sensitivity to climate externalities, with the effect governing long-run rather than short-run emissions and strengthening when investors anticipate tighter regulation. Heightened uncertainty about future climate risks weakens that pressure and can raise emissions. Calibrated to US data, the impact of green investors remains limited at current wealth shares and practices (Angelis et al., 2022).

Taken together, these results define the conditions under which impact claims are credible. Claims are strongest where capital is provided directly to a constrained enterprise, where the counterfactual is documented rather than assumed, where the investor's participation demonstrably changed the terms available, and where outcomes are measured against a baseline established in advance. Claims are weakest where they rest on secondary market holdings, portfolio composition, or output counts unaccompanied by any counterfactual. The distinction is not a matter of degree but of whether the central assertion has been tested at all.

References

Berk, J., & van Binsbergen, J. H. (2024). The impact of impact investing. Journal of Financial Economics, 164, 103972. https://doi.org/10.1016/j.jfineco.2024.103972

De Angelis, T., Tankov, P., & Zerbib, O. (2022). Climate impact investing. Management Science, 69(12), 7669-7692. https://doi.org/10.1287/mnsc.2022.4472

French, M., Kimmitt, J., Wilson, R., Jamieson, D. W., & Lowe, T. (2022). Social impact bonds and public service reform: back to the future of New Public Management? International Public Management Journal, 26(3), 376-395. https://doi.org/10.1080/10967494.2022.2050859

Global Impact Investing Network. (2024). Sizing the Impact Investing Market 2024. Global Impact Investing Network. https://thegiin.org/publication/research/sizing-the-impact-investing-market-2024/

Heeb, F., Kölbel, J. F., Paetzold, F., & Zeisberger, S. (2022). Do investors care about impact? Review of Financial Studies, 36(5), 1737-1787. https://doi.org/10.1093/rfs/hhac066

Hulse, E. S. G., Atun, R., McPake, B., & Lee, J. T. (2021). Use of social impact bonds in financing health systems responses to non-communicable diseases: scoping review. BMJ Global Health, 6(3), e004127. https://doi.org/10.1136/bmjgh-2020-004127

Chapter 6: Blended Finance and Capital Mobilization in Emerging Markets

The investment gap identified in Chapter 1 is not distributed evenly. It concentrates in emerging markets and developing economies, where projects that would be plainly financeable in advanced economies fail to reach financial close. The reason is rarely that the underlying assets are unsound. It is that capital demands a return in these markets which the projects cannot pay, for reasons largely unrelated to the projects themselves. This chapter examines the cost of capital constraint, the concessional instruments designed to address it, the disappointing record of private capital mobilization, proposals to expand multilateral development bank capacity, and the sovereign debt conditions that increasingly determine what is possible.

The Cost of Capital Constraint in Developing Economies

A solar installation with identical technical specifications, capacity factor, and construction cost produces very different electricity prices depending on where it is built, because the cost of capital differs so sharply across jurisdictions. For capital-intensive assets with long lives and negligible fuel costs, financing terms dominate the levelized cost calculation. Renewable generation is the extreme case: almost the entire lifetime cost is incurred upfront, so the discount rate applied to that expenditure determines whether the resulting electricity is cheap or expensive.

The premium demanded in developing economies decomposes into several distinct components that are frequently discussed as a single undifferentiated risk. Sovereign risk reflects the possibility of default, expropriation, or abrupt policy reversal. Currency risk arises where revenues accrue in local currency while financing is denominated in hard currency, and it is often the largest single component. Offtaker credit risk concerns whether the utility purchasing the electricity will pay, which in many markets is a genuine question. Regulatory uncertainty covers tariff revision, permitting, and grid access. Each requires a different mitigation instrument, and treating them as one aggregate risk premium leads directly to mismatched interventions.

Incorporating empirically estimated cost of capital differentiated by country and technology into an ensemble of five climate-energy-economy models quantifies the consequences. Standard transition models do not differentiate regional financing costs and therefore cannot evaluate risk-sharing mechanisms for renewable electricity generation at all. Alleviating financial constraints benefits both climate outcomes and international equity, since risk premium convergence across countries improves energy availability, affordability, and sustainability in the developing world (Calcaterra et al., 2024). The finding that widely used models cannot represent the binding constraint is itself significant, because those models inform the policy debate about what the transition requires.

The consequence for investment geography is stark. Capital concentrates where it is cheap, which is where decarbonization is already most advanced, while the regions with the fastest projected growth in energy demand attract the least. This is not a market failure in the conventional sense. Each individual financing decision is rational given the risks faced; the aggregate outcome is nonetheless one in which the global transition proceeds slowest exactly where future emissions will be greatest.

Concessional Capital and Risk Mitigation Instruments

Blended finance uses public or philanthropic capital to change the risk-return profile of transactions that would not otherwise proceed. The instruments available differ in what they actually do, and selecting among them requires diagnosing which constraint binds.

First-loss and subordinated capital absorbs initial losses, improving the risk position of senior investors without changing the underlying asset. Guarantees transfer specified risks to a creditworthy counterparty, which is efficient when the guarantor's credit is materially stronger than the project's. Political risk insurance covers expropriation, transfer restriction, and breach of contract. Technical assistance funds project preparation, addressing pipeline scarcity rather than risk pricing. Currency hedging facilities address the mismatch directly, which matters because no amount of first-loss capital solves a currency problem.

Instrument selection is frequently mismatched to the binding constraint. Providing first-loss capital to a project whose actual obstacle is an unbankable offtaker addresses a symptom, and providing a guarantee where the real problem is that no viable project has been prepared addresses nothing at all. The consequence is concessional capital deployed without effect, and it is difficult to detect because the transaction may proceed anyway for unrelated reasons.

Currency risk deserves particular attention because it is both the largest component in many transactions and the least well served by available instruments. Long-dated hedging markets in most developing-country currencies are thin or absent, so a fifteen-year renewable project cannot hedge its exposure through conventional means at any reasonable cost. Dedicated facilities exist to provide synthetic long-tenor hedges, but their capacity is small relative to demand and the cost still consumes much of the return. The alternative, local currency lending from institutions able to fund themselves domestically, depends on the depth of domestic capital markets, which is exactly what is missing in the markets where the need is greatest.

The reciprocal risk is subsidizing transactions that would have proceeded regardless. Concessionality discipline requires demonstrating that the concessional element was necessary and was set at the minimum level sufficient, a determination that must be made before the fact and is rarely revisited afterward. Commercial parties have every incentive to accept concessional terms whether or not they need them, and the counterparty assessing necessity is typically the institution whose mandate is measured by deployment volume.

Mobilization Ratios and the Evidence on Leverage

The central claim made for blended finance is leverage: that each unit of public capital mobilizes several units of private capital. Reported mobilization ratios depend heavily on measurement convention, including whether co-financing by other public institutions counts as private mobilization, whether the full transaction value or only the incremental portion is attributed, and how commitments are distinguished from disbursements.

Aggregate flows provide context for what has been achieved. Climate finance provided and mobilized by developed countries reached USD 132.8 billion in 2023 and USD 136.7 billion in 2024, having exceeded the USD 100 billion annual goal for the first time in 2022 at USD 115.9 billion (OECD, 2026). The goal was met, several years later than promised, and the mobilized private share within these totals has consistently fallen short of the multiples anticipated when blended finance gained prominence.

The distribution matters as much as the aggregate. Global climate finance reached an all-time high of USD 1.9 trillion in 2023, with early data indicating flows exceeded USD 2 trillion in 2024. Yet mitigation accounted for USD 1,780 billion against only USD 65 billion for adaptation, and three regions received 79 percent of the total, with China alone capturing 36 percent of global flows. Private climate finance grew at roughly 30 percent annually from 2018 to 2023 against 18 percent for the public sector (Climate Policy Initiative, 2025).

These figures describe a market working well where conditions already favour it and poorly everywhere else. Private capital growth outpacing public growth is frequently cited as evidence that mobilization is succeeding. Read alongside the regional and thematic distribution, it more plausibly indicates that private capital is flowing to mature technologies in creditworthy markets, which requires no mobilization effort at all. Realized mobilization has fallen furthest short in low-income countries and adaptation, precisely the segments where concessional capital was expected to make the greatest difference.

Public finance also flows in directions that work against the stated objective. Mapping public and private financial flows into large-scale petrochemical projects for 2010 to 2020 shows that public finance for petrochemicals is highly globalized and largely originates in developed countries, with lending and guarantees from export credit agencies and development finance institutions playing a central leveraging role. Because the resulting industrial infrastructure is designed to last decades, this financing contributes strongly to sectoral carbon lock-in and constrains the scope for later low-carbon investment (Skovgaard et al., 2023). The same institutional machinery that mobilizes private capital for the transition mobilizes it against the transition, and the two flows are rarely assessed together.

Multilateral Development Bank Reform and Balance Sheet Capacity

Proposals to expand multilateral development bank lending capacity have moved from technical discussion into finance ministry agendas. The mechanisms include revising capital adequacy frameworks to permit higher leverage against existing capital, recognising callable capital as loss-absorbing, issuing hybrid instruments, and using portfolio guarantees to free balance sheet space.

The binding constraint is the AAA credit rating most of these institutions hold, which allows them to borrow cheaply and lend below market rates. Expanded lending increases leverage, and rating agency methodologies penalise leverage. The institutions face a genuine trade-off between lending volume and funding cost, and beyond a threshold, additional lending raises the cost of all their lending. Reform proposals that ignore this constraint mistake a real limit for institutional conservatism, though the calibration of rating methodologies to institutions with preferred creditor status and callable capital is legitimately contested.

Callable capital occupies a particular place in this debate. Shareholders have committed substantial sums payable on demand should an institution face severe distress, and these commitments come overwhelmingly from highly rated sovereigns. Recognising even a portion of callable capital as loss-absorbing would expand lending headroom considerably without new budget appropriations. Rating agencies have been reluctant, on the reasonable ground that a call has never been tested and its speed and political reliability are unknown. The disagreement is not primarily technical: it concerns how much weight to place on a commitment that has never had to be honoured.

Originate-to-distribute models offer a different route. Rather than holding loans to maturity, development banks originate assets, aggregate them into diversified portfolios, and sell them to institutional investors, recycling capital into new lending. This addresses the intermediation mismatch identified in Chapter 1 by converting individually unbankable exposures into rated, scaled instruments that pension funds and insurers can hold. Progress has been slow because it requires standardized documentation, sufficient volume for diversification, and a track record of default and recovery experience that these portfolios have not yet accumulated.

Debt Sustainability, Currency Risk, and Structural Constraints

Climate investment needs arrive at a moment of widespread sovereign debt distress, and the two interact in a reinforcing pattern. Climate vulnerability raises borrowing costs, higher borrowing costs reduce fiscal space, reduced fiscal space constrains adaptation investment, and inadequate adaptation increases vulnerability.

The empirical evidence for this mechanism is now reasonably firm. Systematic investigation of climate vulnerability and sovereign borrowing costs across 46 developing and advanced countries from 1996 to 2016 finds that a subgroup of 25 climate vulnerable developing countries pay on average 1.174 percent more for debt, with forty members of the vulnerable-country grouping paying an estimated USD 62 billion in additional interest from 2007 to 2016 attributable to climate vulnerability. Measures of social readiness reduce bond yields, indicating that adaptation and resilience investment can lower financing costs, while vulnerability itself threatens debt sustainability and can cause financial exclusion (Kling et al., 2025).

Regional evidence supports the same conclusion through a different design. Testing the link between climate change and sovereign risk across Southeast Asian countries using vulnerability and resilience indices with monthly data for 2002 to 2018 finds that greater climate vulnerability has a sizable positive effect on sovereign bond yields, while greater resilience has an offsetting though smaller effect. Higher debt costs hold back investment in public infrastructure and climate adaptation, increase debt sustainability risk, and diminish development prospects (Beirne et al., 2021).

Instruments designed to break this cycle have attracted attention disproportionate to their scale. Analysis of debt-for-nature swaps across 67 countries at risk of debt distress finds these countries hold over 22 percent of global biodiversity priority areas, of which 82.96 percent are unprotected, and that for 35 of them all unprotected priority areas could be protected for a fraction of outstanding debt, with 11 to 13 percent protected in the remainder (Nedopil et al., 2023). The conservation case is strong. The debt relief delivered is modest relative to the obligations these countries carry, and the transactions are complex, slow, and costly to arrange.

Climate-resilient debt clauses represent a cheaper and more scalable intervention. These provisions suspend debt service automatically following a qualifying disaster, converting a liquidity crisis into a deferral without requiring renegotiation at the moment of greatest distress. They cost creditors little in expected terms, since payments are deferred rather than forgiven, and they address a specific failure mode with precision. Their adoption in new issuance has grown, though the outstanding stock of debt without such clauses remains the dominant exposure and cannot be retrofitted without a restructuring event.

This locates the limit of financial engineering. Instruments can reallocate risk among parties willing to bear it, lower financing costs at the margin, and unlock specific transactions that would otherwise fail. They cannot manufacture fiscal space in a country whose debt burden exceeds its capacity to service, nor substitute for the sovereign risk repricing that would follow durable improvements in policy credibility and creditor treatment. The cost of capital gap is ultimately a political and fiscal problem wearing financial clothing, and the instruments examined here address its symptoms with varying success while leaving its cause untouched.

References

Beirne, J., Renzhi, N., & Volz, U. (2021). Bracing for the typhoon: Climate change and sovereign risk in Southeast Asia. Sustainable Development, 29(3), 537-551. https://doi.org/10.1002/sd.2199

Calcaterra, M., Reis, L. A., Fragkos, P., Briera, T., de Boer, H. S., Egli, F., Emmerling, J., Iyer, G., Mittal, S., Polzin, F., Sanders, M., Schmidt, T. S., Serebriakova, A., Steffen, B., Van de Ven, D. J., van Vuuren, D. P., Waidelich, P., & Tavoni, M. (2024). Reducing the cost of capital to finance the energy transition in developing countries. Nature Energy, 9(10), 1241-1251. https://doi.org/10.1038/s41560-024-01606-7

Climate Policy Initiative. (2025). Global Landscape of Climate Finance 2025. Climate Policy Initiative. https://www.climatepolicyinitiative.org/publication/global-landscape-of-climate-finance-2025/

Kling, G., Lo, Y. C., Murinde, V., & Volz, U. (2025). Climate vulnerability and the cost of debt. Oxford Open Economics, 4. https://doi.org/10.1093/ooec/odaf003

Nedopil, C., Yue, M., & Hughes, A. C. (2023). Are debt-for-nature swaps scalable: Which nature, how much debt, and who pays? AMBIO, 53(1), 63-78. https://doi.org/10.1007/s13280-023-01914-4

OECD. (2026). Climate Finance Provided and Mobilised by Developed Countries in 2013-2024. OECD. https://www.oecd.org/en/publications/climate-finance-provided-and-mobilised-by-developed-countries-in-2013-2024_ab5eb9ad-en.html

Skovgaard, J., Finkill, G., Bauer, F., Åhman, M., & Nielsen, T. (2023). Finance for fossils – The role of public financing in expanding petrochemicals. Global Environmental Change, 80, 102657. https://doi.org/10.1016/j.gloenvcha.2023.102657

Chapter 7: Compliance Carbon Markets and Emissions Pricing

Carbon pricing addresses the externality identified in Chapter 1 directly rather than through disclosure, labeling, or investor preference. By attaching a cost to emissions, it changes the relative economics of emitting and abating for every participant in a covered market, whether or not any of them holds a view about climate change. This chapter examines the design of emissions trading systems, the allocation choices that determine their distributional and incentive properties, carbon taxation as an alternative instrument, the extension of domestic pricing into trade policy through border adjustment, and the aggregate record of what pricing has achieved.

Design Architecture of Emissions Trading Systems

An emissions trading system caps aggregate emissions from covered installations, issues allowances equal to that cap, and permits trading so that abatement occurs where it is cheapest. The design parameters that determine performance are coverage, cap trajectory, compliance period length, provisions for banking and borrowing allowances across periods, and mechanisms controlling price volatility.

Coverage determines reach. Most systems begin with large stationary sources in power generation and heavy industry, where emissions are concentrated and monitoring is straightforward, and extend later to transport, buildings, and aviation. Each extension increases abatement potential and administrative complexity together, and sectors with many small emitters are frequently addressed through upstream coverage of fuel suppliers rather than downstream coverage of users.

Banking allows participants to carry surplus allowances forward, smoothing prices across periods and rewarding early abatement. Borrowing from future periods provides flexibility at the cost of weakening the near-term constraint, and most systems restrict it tightly. The accumulated bank of allowances becomes a significant policy variable in its own right: a large surplus depresses prices for years regardless of the current cap, which is what prompted the introduction of quantity-based reserve mechanisms that adjust auction volumes in response to allowances in circulation.

The cap trajectory carries more weight than any other parameter, since it determines the scarcity that gives allowances value. Early systems set caps against projected business-as-usual emissions that proved too generous when economic conditions changed, producing prolonged periods of near-zero prices and lasting damage to the instrument's credibility. Later designs have tightened by applying a linear reduction factor to historical emissions, sometimes with mid-course adjustments that accelerate the decline. The lesson from the first generation is that a cap set with reference to forecast emissions inherits the forecast's error, while a cap set as a declining path from observed emissions does not.

Price containment mechanisms sit uneasily with the logic of quantity control. A pure cap fixes emissions and lets prices vary; introducing a price floor or ceiling converts the instrument into a hybrid whose emissions outcome is no longer fixed. Floors protect against collapse in the abatement signal when demand falls, and they have proved important where economic shocks or overlapping renewable support policies would otherwise leave the cap non-binding. The trade-off is explicit: certainty about price is purchased with uncertainty about quantity.

Allocation Methods, Leakage, and Competitiveness Protection

How allowances reach participants does not affect the environmental outcome, since the cap is fixed either way, but it determines who bears the cost and what secondary incentives are created. Auctioning requires participants to purchase allowances, generating public revenue and exposing them to the full price. Free allocation distributes allowances at no cost, typically benchmarked against production so that efficient installations receive more than they need and inefficient ones fall short.

Free allocation is justified by the risk of carbon leakage: production migrating to jurisdictions without comparable carbon costs, relocating rather than reducing emissions while damaging domestic industry. The empirical evidence for leakage at observed carbon prices has generally been weaker than the volume of protection provided would suggest, in part because free allocation has been calibrated to assumed rather than demonstrated risk, and in part because carbon costs remain small relative to other determinants of industrial location such as energy prices, labour, and proximity to markets.

The fiscal cost of this protection is substantial, since every freely allocated allowance is revenue foregone. Its effect on abatement incentives is subtler. Benchmarked free allocation tied to output preserves the marginal incentive to reduce emissions intensity, because a firm still profits from selling surplus allowances, but it weakens the incentive to reduce output or shift demand toward less carbon-intensive substitutes. It also insulates consumers from the price signal, so the demand-side response that carbon pricing is meant to trigger largely does not occur in protected sectors.

Quantifying the alternatives clarifies the trade-off. Analysis comparing an import-only border adjustment, a symmetric border adjustment covering imports and exports, and an excise on embodied emissions combined with continued free allocation, using product-level carbon intensity estimates for 4,400 commodity groups, finds that around 10 percent of EU exports and 5 percent of domestic manufacturing sales meet carbon leakage risk criteria under an incomplete border adjustment at 30 euros per tonne. The distributional implications of consistent carbon pricing of basic materials are small and progressive, and an excise on embodied emissions could generate revenues of around 20 billion euros for climate action (Stede et al., 2021). Protection at current levels appears considerably broader than measured risk warrants.

Carbon Taxes, Price Levels, and Revenue Use

A carbon tax fixes the price and lets emissions adjust, the mirror image of a cap. The choice between instruments turns on which uncertainty is more tolerable. Where the marginal damage from an additional tonne is relatively flat but abatement costs are uncertain, price certainty is preferable because it avoids imposing unexpectedly high costs. Where a specific emissions budget must be met, quantity control is preferable.

Practical considerations often matter more than this theoretical comparison. Taxes are administratively simpler, particularly when levied upstream on fuel supply, requiring no allowance registry, auction infrastructure, or market oversight. They generate predictable revenue, which assists fiscal planning. Trading systems, by contrast, have proved more politically durable in several jurisdictions precisely because free allocation allows the initial burden on incumbents to be softened, an option a tax does not offer without explicit and visible exemptions.

Observed price levels sit well below most estimates of what temperature-aligned pathways require, and the gap is widest in the sectors hardest to abate. Analysis of emissions-intensive, trade-exposed sectors including aluminium, cement, chemicals, iron and steel, lime, pulp and paper, and petroleum refining finds that existing carbon pricing has had limited impact because marginal abatement costs in these sectors almost always exceed the tax rate or allowance price. Emissions trading systems with free allocation have minimized adverse economic impacts and associated leakage, but since internationally coordinated policies are unlikely, more ambitious domestic policies create leakage risk that must be managed through packages differentiated between producers competing with imports and producers serving export markets. Carbon pricing remains a critical component of each package because it limits economic harm, supports innovation, and generates revenue that can compensate adversely affected groups and build public support (Haites et al., 2023).

Public acceptance is shaped less by the price level than by beliefs about where the money goes and whether the burden is fairly shared. Opposition frequently rests on the expectation that revenue will disappear into general government spending, and on the perception that carbon pricing burdens households with limited ability to substitute, such as rural residents dependent on private vehicles. Both concerns are addressable through design rather than through communication, and systems that made revenue treatment explicit and visible at the outset have proved more durable than those that treated it as a secondary fiscal matter.

Revenue use is where carbon pricing's political durability is largely determined. Options include lump-sum dividends returning revenue to households, reductions in other taxes, and earmarked spending on climate programmes. Dividends make the progressive incidence of carbon pricing visible, since low-income households typically receive more than they pay. Earmarking builds constituencies with a stake in continuation. Global carbon pricing revenues exceeded USD 100 billion in 2024, with over half of the revenue generated for public budgets earmarked for environment, infrastructure, and development spending (World Bank, 2025).

Carbon Border Adjustment and Trade Interaction

Border carbon adjustment extends a domestic carbon price to imported goods, charging importers for embodied emissions and crediting any carbon price already paid in the country of production. The stated purpose is to permit domestic ambition without leakage, replacing free allocation with a mechanism that maintains the price signal for domestic consumers while equalising treatment of foreign competitors.

Implementation is demanding. Calculating embodied emissions in an imported product requires data from foreign producers whose reporting infrastructure may not exist, and default values applied in the absence of verified data must be set high enough to encourage reporting without being punitive. Crediting foreign carbon prices requires judgments about whether another jurisdiction's instrument is equivalent, which is a diplomatic question as much as a technical one. Coverage limited to a few basic materials avoids much of this complexity while leaving downstream products, where much embodied carbon actually resides, outside the mechanism.

The distributional consequences fall predominantly on countries least able to absorb them. Assessment of country-level exposure under a sectoral scenario and an economy-wide scenario, using a risk index combining export structure, emissions intensity, reduction targets, and institutional monitoring capacity, finds that impacts are distributed unevenly and that most high-risk countries are located in Africa under both scenarios. Institutional capacity for monitoring, reporting, and verification emerges as a central determinant of exposure, and case studies of Mozambique, Bosnia and Herzegovina, and Morocco identify distinct vulnerability patterns (Eicke et al., 2021).

Trade network analysis reaches a compatible conclusion while pointing toward a remedy. Applying a throughflow-based accounting method to detailed trade data to compare implementation options finds that middle- and low-income countries for which the EU is an important export market would be disproportionately impacted even under conservative implementations, and that the mechanism channels the domestic carbon price outward to trading partners. International revenue recycling schemes could make the mechanism more inclusive toward vulnerable countries and support global climate cooperation (Beaufils et al., 2023). Whether such recycling occurs is a political choice that determines whether border adjustment is read abroad as climate policy or as protectionism.

Coverage, Effectiveness, and the Limits of Price Instruments

The aggregate picture is one of substantial institutional expansion producing modest emissions effect. Around 28 percent of global greenhouse gas emissions are now covered by a carbon price, with

80 instruments in operation worldwide, a net increase of five over the year. Over the past decade average prices have nearly doubled and coverage has grown from 12 percent to 28 percent, and all large middle-income economies have implemented or are considering direct carbon pricing (World Bank, 2025). Coverage of roughly a quarter of global emissions means three-quarters remain unpriced.

Where pricing has been evaluated rigorously, it works. Using China's regional pilots as a quasi-natural experiment with a matched difference-in-differences design applied to firm tax records in manufacturing and public utilities for 2009 to 2015 shows a 16.7 percent reduction in total firm emissions and a 9.7 percent reduction in emission intensity. Firms abated by conserving energy and switching to low-carbon fuels. Economic effects were mixed, with negative effects on employment and capital input alongside improved productivity and no significant effect on output or exports. Effects varied notably across pilots, with mass-based allocation rules, higher prices, and active trading producing more pronounced abatement (Cui et al., 2021).

That last finding is the practical lesson. The instrument's effectiveness depends on design choices that many systems have made poorly, and a system with generous free allocation, a loose cap, and illiquid trading will produce little abatement while still being counted among the world's carbon pricing instruments.

Attributing emissions reductions to pricing rather than to complementary policy is methodologically demanding, which is why rigorous evaluations remain scarce relative to the number of systems in operation. Most jurisdictions with carbon pricing simultaneously operate renewable support schemes, efficiency standards, and coal phase-out commitments, each of which reduces emissions and each of which reduces demand for allowances. Where a cap binds, complementary policies displace abatement rather than adding to it, since the cap fixes total emissions regardless. Where the cap does not bind, complementary policies drive the observed reductions while the carbon price receives the credit. Disentangling the two requires a credible counterfactual, and the studies that construct one convincingly are few.

Price signals also reach some abatement options far better than others. They work well where a substitute exists and the decision-maker faces the price directly, as in fuel switching in electricity generation. They work poorly where abatement requires replacing capital stock with technology that is not yet cost-competitive at any plausible price, as in primary steel and cement, and where split incentives prevent the price reaching the decision-maker, as in rented buildings. In these cases pricing is necessary but insufficient, and the complementary instruments required are the subject of Chapter 9. The voluntary markets examined next attempt to extend carbon pricing into the three-quarters of emissions that compliance systems do not reach, and the difficulties they encounter are instructive about why that extension is harder than it appears.

References

Beaufils, T., Ward, H., Jakob, M., & Wenz, L. (2023). Assessing different European Carbon Border Adjustment Mechanism implementations and their impact on trade partners. Communications Earth & Environment, 4(1). https://doi.org/10.1038/s43247-023-00788-4

Cui, J., Wang, C., Zhang, J., & Zheng, Y. (2021). The effectiveness of China's regional carbon market pilots in reducing firm emissions. Proceedings of the National Academy of Sciences, 118(52). https://doi.org/10.1073/pnas.2109912118

Eicke, L., Weko, S., Apergi, M., & Marian, A. (2021). Pulling up the carbon ladder? Decarbonization, dependence, and third-country risks from the European carbon border adjustment mechanism. Energy Research & Social Science, 80, 102240. https://doi.org/10.1016/j.erss.2021.102240

Haites, E., Bertoldi, P., König, M., Bataille, C., Creutzig, F., Dasgupta, D., de la Rue du Can, S., Khennas, S., Kim, Y. G., Nilsson, L. J., Roy, J., & Sari, A. P. (2023). Contribution of carbon pricing to meeting a mid-century net zero target. Climate Policy, 24(1), 1-12. https://doi.org/10.1080/14693062.2023.2170312

Stede, J., Pauliuk, S., Hardadi, G., & Neuhoff, K. (2021). Carbon pricing of basic materials: Incentives and risks for the value chain and consumers. Ecological Economics, 189, 107168. https://doi.org/10.1016/j.ecolecon.2021.107168

World Bank. (2025). State and Trends of Carbon Pricing 2025. World Bank. https://openknowledge.worldbank.org/entities/publication/e5f6e755-e6a6-4d2c-927a-23b5cc8a9b03

Chapter 8: Voluntary Carbon Markets, Integrity, and Article 6 Cooperation

Compliance carbon pricing reaches roughly a quarter of global emissions. Voluntary carbon markets were built to extend a price into the remainder, allowing companies to fund abatement wherever it is cheapest and to claim the resulting reductions against their own targets. The mechanism depends entirely on whether a purchased credit represents a tonne of emissions that would otherwise have entered the atmosphere. This chapter examines how credits are generated, the integrity failures documented across major project categories, the governance response, the distinct market for durable removals, and how Article 6 of the Paris Agreement restructures the relationship between voluntary claims and sovereign accounting.

Credit Generation, Methodologies, and Market Structure

A carbon credit begins with a methodology: a standardized procedure specifying how a project type establishes its baseline, monitors performance, and calculates reductions. Standard-setting bodies approve methodologies, project developers design activities to fit them, independent validation bodies confirm the design conforms, and after implementation verification bodies confirm the claimed reductions occurred. Credits are then issued into a registry, transferred through intermediaries, and eventually retired against a buyer's claim.

The structure resembles financial auditing and carries a similar conflict. Validation and verification bodies are selected and paid by project developers, who benefit from favorable determinations. Unlike financial audit, this activity operates without statutory backing in most jurisdictions, and the standard-setting bodies that accredit verifiers are themselves funded by issuance fees, giving them a financial interest in credit volume. Every actor in the chain other than the buyer is compensated in proportion to credits created.

Methodology approval deserves particular scrutiny because it determines everything downstream. Once a methodology is approved, projects conforming to it are credited more or less mechanically, so an error in the methodology propagates across every project using it. Revising an approved methodology is slow and contested, since developers have made investments predicated on the existing rules and registries face claims that retroactive tightening is unfair. The result is that methodological weaknesses identified by researchers can persist for years while credits continue to be issued against them.

Market structure amplifies opacity. Most transactions occur bilaterally over the counter rather than on exchanges, so prices are not systematically observable and differ enormously across project types, vintages, and geographies. Intermediaries purchase portfolios and resell them, sometimes several times, and the margin captured between project developer and final buyer can be a substantial share of the price. A buyer paying a high price has limited assurance that the additional payment reached the activity generating the credit.

Additionality, Baselines, and Permanence

Three technical requirements determine whether a credit is real. Additionality requires that the abatement would not have occurred without the revenue the credits provide. Baselines require a defensible counterfactual against which reductions are measured. Permanence requires that the carbon stays out of the atmosphere, which matters acutely for land-based projects where stored carbon can be released by fire, disease, harvesting, or policy change.

Each requirement is difficult, and baseline construction is where failures have concentrated. Evaluation of California's forest carbon offsets program, digitising comprehensive project records and analysing them against detailed forest inventory data, demonstrates the mechanism by which a plausible design produces systematic error. Crediting projects against coarse regional carbon averages allows developers to select forests that are ecologically distinct from those averages, and this adverse selection produced over-crediting of 30.0 million tonnes of carbon dioxide equivalent, or 29.4 percent of the credits analyzed, worth an estimated USD 410 million at market prices. The program creates incentives to generate credits that do not reflect real climate benefits rather than to improve forest management (Badgley et al., 2021).

The problem is not confined to one program. A review of the scientific literature on additionality, baselines, leakage, durability, and forest carbon accounting, assessed against the protocols governing improved forest management projects that have produced 11 percent of all voluntary registry credits, finds that protocols deviate from scientific understanding on baselines, leakage, reversal risk, and the accounting of carbon in harvested wood products. These deviations risk significant over-estimation of issued credits, and while more conservative baselines would substantially reduce over-crediting risk, they would not resolve it (Haya et al., 2023).

Demand-side behavior compounds supply-side weakness rather than disciplining it. Examination of the twenty companies retiring the most offsets between 2020 and 2023, assessed across project risk type, project and credit age, price, and country of implementation, finds that 87 percent of purchased offsets carry a high risk of not delivering real and additional reductions, with most originating from forest conservation and renewable energy projects, and most failing to meet industry standards on age and country of implementation. Companies predominantly sourced cheap, low-quality credits (Trencher et al., 2024).

This finding is important because it locates responsibility. A market where the largest buyers systematically select the cheapest credits generates no price premium for quality, and without such a premium, developers have no commercial reason to bear the additional cost of conservative baselines and rigorous monitoring. The integrity problem is not solely a failure of standards; it is sustained by what buyers are willing to pay for.

Integrity Initiatives and Market Governance Response

The governance response has proceeded along two tracks. Supply-side initiatives define what constitutes a high-quality credit, and demand-side guidance defines what claims a buyer may legitimately make. Together they attempt to establish a quality tier distinguishable from the undifferentiated market.

The principal supply-side effort establishes threshold criteria and assesses carbon-crediting programmes and credit categories against them. The assessment framework elaborates criteria for evaluating credits and programmes against ten core principles covering disclosure, sustainable development, and emissions integrity, with the purpose of identifying credits producing real, additional, and verifiable climate impact. Following first decisions in May 2024, the governing board approved 40 crediting methodologies as meeting requirements and found that 25 did not (Integrity Council for the Voluntary Carbon Market, 2024).

That approval rate is itself informative. A regime rejecting roughly a third of assessed methodologies is applying a meaningful filter, and the rejections have concentrated in the categories where the academic literature identified the deepest problems. The consequence is a market segmenting into a smaller high-integrity tier and a residual pool of credits that remain issued, tradable, and in many cases still purchased.

Demand-side guidance addresses a different failure, namely what a buyer may claim. The distinction between funding mitigation beyond one's value chain and asserting that one's own emissions have been neutralised is substantial, and the language of carbon neutrality obscured it for years. Contribution claims, in which a company states that it financed emissions reductions without asserting neutralisation, describe the underlying transaction more accurately and are correspondingly less attractive to marketing departments. Reversal risk is managed through buffer pools, in which a share of credits from each project is withheld to cover future losses, though buffer sizing has generally been set by convention rather than by measured reversal rates.

Whether this restores confidence or simply narrows the market is unresolved. Corporate buyers facing reputational risk have in several cases withdrawn from offsetting entirely rather than navigate quality assessment, shifting toward direct emissions reductions and, where they retain offsetting, toward higher-priced removals. That response is defensible for the individual buyer while reducing the finance flowing to conservation activities that, whatever their crediting flaws, were funding real protection. Tightening integrity standards has an environmental cost as well as a benefit, and the net effect depends on what displaced capital does instead.

Carbon Dioxide Removal and Durable Credit Markets

Removals differ fundamentally from avoidance. An avoidance credit claims that emissions did not occur; a removal credit claims that carbon dioxide was taken from the atmosphere and stored. Only removals can neutralise residual emissions in a net zero framework, which is why the two are increasingly treated as separate markets with separate prices.

Durability is the property that determines whether a removal is fit for that purpose, and it has been treated far too loosely. Modeling carbon dioxide removal with varying storage durations shows that with 100-year storage and 6 gigatonnes of residual annual emissions, net zero produces 0.8 degrees Celsius of additional warming by 2500 relative to permanent storage. Storage periods shorter than 1000 years are insufficient to neutralise remaining fossil emissions, and credible neutralisation requires matching emissions with removals of similar atmospheric residence time and storage reservoir. Existing interpretations of durable storage have ranged from decades to millennia (Brunner et al., 2024).

This has a direct implication for market design. A forestry removal with a hundred-year permanence guarantee and a geological storage removal are not interchangeable units, and treating them as fungible tonnes within a single market understates the warming consequence of the former. Matching the storage reservoir to the emission source is a physical requirement rather than an accounting preference.

The regulatory treatment of removals remains fragmented. A review of how removals are handled across compliance and voluntary markets, covering baseline-and-credit and cap-and-trade systems, finds that the Kyoto mechanisms and major voluntary standards long focused on biological removals lacking inherent permanence, developing methodologies for geological storage, mineralisation, and biochar only recently. New entrants generating removal credits frequently disregard safeguards such as additionality, credit prices span three orders of magnitude from 1 to 1000, and volumes range from hundreds to tens of millions of credits. Absent a coordinated approach, the current conditions risk scandals that would taint the removal market as a whole (Michaelowa et al., 2023).

Advance purchase agreements have become the principal financing mechanism for early-stage removal technologies, with buyers committing to future delivery at prices far above prevailing credit prices to fund capacity that does not yet exist. This resembles venture financing more than credit purchase, and the buyer bears technology risk alongside delivery risk. It also concentrates the market in a small number of well-capitalised purchasers whose procurement decisions effectively determine which removal technologies receive the capital to reach commercial scale.

Article 6 Cooperation and Sovereign Carbon Accounting

Article 6 of the Paris Agreement changes the accounting context in which all of this operates. Under the predecessor regime, developing countries had no emissions targets, so credits generated there could be sold abroad without affecting any national account. Under the Paris framework every country has a nationally determined contribution, which means a tonne reduced in one country and claimed by a buyer in another must be subtracted from the host country's own account to avoid being counted twice.

That subtraction is the corresponding adjustment, and it converts credit export into a real fiscal decision. A host country authorising a transfer gives up abatement it could have counted toward its own target and must find replacement abatement elsewhere. Cheap domestic abatement that once looked like an export opportunity now looks like an asset a country may prefer to retain, and this recognition has made authorisation regimes considerably more restrictive than early market projections assumed.

Two channels operate. Article 6.2 permits bilateral cooperation with internationally transferred mitigation outcomes governed by agreements between participating countries. Article 6.4 establishes a centralised crediting mechanism under international supervision with standardized methodologies. Both require host country authorisation for credits carrying a corresponding adjustment, and this has bifurcated the voluntary market into authorised credits usable toward national or international compliance claims and unauthorised credits that support only unregulated corporate claims.

The pricing consequences follow directly. Authorised credits carry the host country's opportunity cost and command a premium; unauthorised credits do not and are correspondingly cheaper, but the claims they support are weaker and increasingly contested. Supply of authorised credits depends on sovereign decisions rather than on project economics, which introduces a constraint no amount of methodological improvement can relax.

What emerges is a market whose fundamental problem was never primarily technical. Baselines can be tightened, monitoring improved, and permanence better specified, and each reform raises credit quality and cost together. The deeper issue is that the market's demand side has consistently rewarded cheapness over integrity, while its supply side now depends on sovereign willingness to forgo domestic abatement. Voluntary carbon markets can finance genuine mitigation where those conditions are met. They cannot substitute for the compliance pricing examined in Chapter 7, and treating them as a lower-cost alternative to abatement within a buyer's own operations remains the central error the integrity reforms are attempting to correct.

References

Badgley, G., Freeman, J., Hamman, J., Haya, B., Trugman, A. T., Anderegg, W. R. L., & Cullenward, D. (2021). Systematic over-crediting in California's forest carbon offsets program. Global Change Biology, 28(4), 1433-1445. https://doi.org/10.1111/gcb.15943

Brunner, C., Hausfather, Z., & Knutti, R. (2024). Durability of carbon dioxide removal is critical for Paris climate goals. Communications Earth & Environment, 5(1). https://doi.org/10.1038/s43247-024-01808-7

Haya, B., Evans, S. L., Brown, L. B., Bukoski, J. J., Butsic, V., Cabiyo, B., Jacobson, R., Kerr, A., Potts, M. D., & Sanchez, D. L. (2023). Comprehensive review of carbon quantification by improved forest management offset protocols. Frontiers in Forests and Global Change, 6. https://doi.org/10.3389/ffgc.2023.958879

Integrity Council for the Voluntary Carbon Market. (2024). Core Carbon Principles, Assessment Framework and Assessment Procedure. Integrity Council for the Voluntary Carbon Market. https://icvcm.org/assessment-framework/

Michaelowa, A., Honegger, M., Poralla, M., Winkler, M., Dalfiume, S., & Nayak, A. (2023). International carbon markets for carbon dioxide removal. PLOS Climate, 2(5), e0000118. https://doi.org/10.1371/journal.pclm.0000118

Trencher, G., Nick, S., Carlson, J., & Johnson, M. R. (2024). Demand for low-quality offsets by major companies undermines climate integrity of the voluntary carbon market. Nature Communications, 15(1), 6863. https://doi.org/10.1038/s41467-024-51151-w

Chapter 9: Transition Finance and the Future Financial Architecture

The mechanisms examined so far share a common bias. They direct capital efficiently toward assets that are already commercially viable, in jurisdictions where capital is already cheap, for activities whose benefits can be captured as revenue. What they reach poorly is heavy industry that must replace capital stock before its technology is competitive, adaptation whose benefit is an avoided loss rather than a sold service, and ecosystems whose value resists monetization entirely. This chapter examines the instruments and institutional changes intended to address those gaps, and assesses which structural changes are plausible over the coming decade.

Transition Finance for Emissions-Intensive Sectors

Steel, cement, chemicals, shipping, and aviation present a financing problem distinct from anything in the preceding chapters. Abatement in these sectors requires replacing long-lived capital equipment with technology that costs more to build and more to operate, producing an identical physical product at a higher price. There is no efficiency gain to fund the investment and no consumer willingness to pay a premium for structurally identical materials. The gap between conventional and low-carbon production must be closed by policy, procurement, or subsidy, or it does not close.

The scale of coordination required is visible in sectoral planning. Analysis of 29 industry transition roadmaps across 13 countries, spanning extractive, processing, and end-use heavy industry sectors, compares decarbonization ambition, implementation cost, and mitigation measures, and finds that global efforts remain insufficiently aligned. Implementation encounters common and comparable barriers across different industries and countries, with financial cost recurring as a constraint throughout, which points toward international cooperation and structured knowledge sharing as prerequisites rather than enhancements (Johnson et al., 2021).

Transition finance attempts to fund exactly this activity, and it collides with the classification problem identified in Chapter 2. A loan financing a steel plant's conversion to direct reduction is financing one of the most emissions-intensive assets in any portfolio, and under most taxonomies and portfolio alignment metrics it will register as such for years before the benefit appears. Instruments designed to reward low measured emissions actively discourage the transactions that deliver the largest absolute abatement.

Credible criteria for financing high-emitting activity therefore have to rest on trajectory rather than on current performance. This requires an entity-level transition plan specifying capital expenditure commitments, technology choices, interim milestones, and governance accountability, assessed for credibility rather than accepted as stated. The evidentiary difficulty identified in Chapter 3 applies directly: assessing whether a plan is credible requires judgment about technology costs and policy durability over decades, and different assessors reach different conclusions. Managed phase-out financing, in which capital funds the early retirement of an emissions-intensive asset rather than its continued operation, faces the same assessment problem alongside the awkward reality that the transaction's success is measured by an asset ceasing to produce.

Adaptation and Resilience Finance

Adaptation attracts a small fraction of climate finance, and the reason is structural rather than attitudinal. Mitigation produces a saleable output: electricity, fuel, or materials generating contracted revenue that supports debt service. Adaptation produces an avoided loss. A sea wall, a drainage upgrade, or a drought-resistant cropping system prevents damage that would otherwise occur, and prevented damage generates no cash flow from which an investor can be repaid. The benefits are also diffuse and largely public, accruing to everyone protected regardless of whether they contributed.

The quantified gap is stark. Adaptation finance needs in developing countries are estimated at USD 310 billion per year by 2035 on modeled costs, or USD 365 billion when based on extrapolation from country plans, against international public adaptation finance flows of USD 26 billion in 2023, leaving needs 12 to 14 times current flows. Most countries now have at least one adaptation policy, strategy, or plan in place, indicating that the planning constraint has eased while the financing constraint has not, and on current trends the goal of doubling international public adaptation finance will not be achieved (UNEP, 2025).

Reframing the problem improves the diagnosis. Examination of the Green Climate Fund's portfolio of 74 adaptation projects shows that two are categorized as private sector projects and nine mobilize private co-finance, while an additional 60 engage the private sector in ways standard finance indicators do not capture. Ordinal regression finds that addressing the market imperfections of positive externalities, imperfect financial markets, and asymmetric information significantly increases private engagement, which shifts attention from removing barriers to correcting the underlying market failures. The analysis also notes that mobilizing private engagement is a means rather than an end, with societal adaptation the actual objective (Stoll et al., 2021).

Measurement compounds the revenue problem. Demonstrating that an adaptation investment worked requires establishing what damage would have occurred without it, which is the counterfactual difficulty examined in Chapter 5 applied to events that may not occur for decades. A drainage system that prevents flooding produces no observable outcome at all in the years when no severe rainfall arrives. Investors and public budgets alike find it harder to justify expenditure whose success is indistinguishable from an absence of trouble, and this asymmetry has consistently favoured mitigation projects with countable outputs over adaptation projects with avoided ones.

Instruments that convert avoided losses into cash flows offer partial solutions. Parametric insurance pays out on a measured trigger such as wind speed or rainfall deficit rather than on assessed damage, allowing rapid disbursement and transferring risk to reinsurance markets. Resilience bonds attempt to capture the insurance premium reduction that resilience investment generates and direct it toward financing that investment. Both operate at modest scale relative to need, and neither changes the fundamental position that most adaptation is a public good requiring public balance sheets.

Nature, Biodiversity, and Natural Capital Finance

Extending sustainable finance to nature raises measurement problems more severe than those in carbon accounting. Carbon has a single unit that is fungible across locations. Biodiversity does not: a hectare of restored wetland and a hectare of protected forest support different species performing different ecological functions, and no defensible exchange rate converts one into the other. Constructing a tradable credit requires exactly such an exchange rate, which is why biodiversity credit markets remain small and contested.

Financial markets have nonetheless begun to price nature-related exposure, though the mechanism is regulatory anticipation rather than ecological assessment. Introducing a corporate biodiversity footprint measure and testing whether it is priced across an international sample of stocks finds that on average it does not explain the cross-section of returns between 2019 and 2022, but that a footprint premium began emerging in October 2021 following the Kunming Declaration, with high-footprint stocks losing value in the days afterward and the launch of the Taskforce on Nature-related Financial Disclosures producing a similar effect. Investors appear to require a risk premium in anticipation of future regulation or litigation (Garel et al., 2024).

That is a meaningful finding about how anticipated policy transmits into asset prices, and it also indicates the limits of disclosure-led approaches. The premium reflects expectations about regulation rather than assessment of ecological damage, so it would respond to a change in political signals regardless of what happens to ecosystems.

Caution about market-based approaches is warranted on governance grounds as well. Drawing on research into the effectiveness, governance, and practice of nature-based solutions, analysis of financing them primarily through natural capital markets finds that a narrow focus carries greenwashing risk, that market mechanisms help bridge the biodiversity funding gap without being sufficient to scale nature-based solutions, and that they present significant governance challenges while risking further entrenchment of power asymmetries. Complementary funding mechanisms are needed alongside market instruments, and nature-based solutions must not displace attention from reducing fossil fuel emissions (Chausson et al., 2023).

Nature finance also interacts directly with the land-based carbon markets examined in Chapter 8, since the same hectares generate both carbon and biodiversity claims. Stacking credits raises double-counting questions that neither market has resolved.

Financial Architecture Reform and Systemic Capacity

Proposals to expand the supply of concessional and long-term capital have converged on a recognisable agenda: rechannelling special drawing rights toward vulnerable economies, international levies on aviation, shipping, or fossil fuel extraction, the capital adequacy reforms examined in Chapter 6, and revision of credit rating methodologies that many argue systematically overstate risk in developing economies.

Credit rating methodology deserves particular attention because its effects are pervasive and largely invisible. Sovereign ratings determine borrowing costs directly and propagate into corporate ratings through the sovereign ceiling, so a rating that overstates risk raises the cost of capital for every borrower in that jurisdiction simultaneously. Critics argue that methodologies weight recent volatility and institutional indicators in ways that penalise developing economies beyond what default histories justify, and that climate vulnerability is incorporated as a risk factor while adaptation investment receives no offsetting recognition. Rating agencies respond that their records are empirically calibrated and that adjusting them on developmental grounds would compromise their analytical basis. The dispute is unresolved, and its resolution would move more capital than most instruments discussed in this book.

Each proposal is technically feasible and politically obstructed, and the obstruction follows a consistent pattern. Measures requiring new appropriations from creditor-country budgets face domestic fiscal constraints. Measures requiring changes to institutional governance face resistance from shareholders whose influence would be diluted. Measures requiring international coordination face the difficulty that any single jurisdiction adopting a levy alone disadvantages its own industry. The proposals that have advanced furthest are those requiring no new money and no governance change, which is also why their aggregate effect is modest.

Set against the investment requirement established in Chapter 1, realistic capacity expansion falls well short. Balance sheet optimization across multilateral institutions might generate additional lending capacity in the low hundreds of billions over a decade. Special drawing rights rechannelling operates at a similar order of magnitude. These are meaningful sums that do not approach the trillions the transition requires in developing economies, which means the architecture debate is about improving terms and lowering costs at the margin rather than about closing the gap through public capital.

Strategic Directions for Capital Allocation

Four conditions determine whether capital reallocation accelerates, and they are not equally addressed by current effort.

Policy credibility matters most. Investors commit capital to twenty-year assets on the basis of expected policy over that horizon, and the value of a carbon price, a subsidy, or a mandate is discounted by the probability of reversal. This is why durability of political commitment affects investment more than the stringency of any individual instrument, and why the reversibility documented in several jurisdictions has raised required returns across the board.

Price signal durability follows from the same logic. The evidence in Chapter 7 indicates that carbon pricing works where it is designed well and applied consistently, and that its principal weakness is coverage rather than mechanism. Extending coverage beyond a quarter of global emissions would do more for allocation than any refinement of disclosure or labeling.

Disclosure quality matters, but as a precondition rather than a driver. The evidence in Chapters 2 and 3 supports a modest claim: standardized information makes comparison possible and constrains false claims, without reliably changing where capital goes.

Cost of capital convergence matters most for the geography of the transition. As Chapters 1 and 6 established, the binding constraint in developing economies is the risk premium rather than the availability of savings or projects, and instruments that compress that premium at scale would shift more capital than every voluntary mechanism in this book combined.

The sequencing implied by this ordering is unfashionable but defensible. Mandatory, universal mechanisms that alter relative returns should take priority over voluntary mechanisms that depend on investor preference, because the latter are bounded by the wealth share of participating investors while the former are not. Risk mitigation instruments that lower the cost of capital in high-premium jurisdictions should take priority over instruments that fine-tune allocation in markets where capital is already cheap and abundant. Public balance sheets should be directed toward the activities private capital structurally cannot fund, principally adaptation and early-stage technology, rather than toward crowding into mature renewable assets that attract commercial financing unaided.

Read as a system rather than as a set of products, sustainable finance has built considerable infrastructure for observing and classifying capital, and comparatively little for changing its price. The distinction drawn in the introduction between mechanisms that alter measurement and mechanisms that alter allocation holds across every chapter of this book. The next decade will determine whether the second category grows to match the first.

References

Chausson, A., Welden, E. A., Melanidis, M. S., Gray, E., Hirons, M., & Seddon, N. (2023). Going beyond market-based mechanisms to finance nature-based solutions and foster sustainable futures. PLOS Climate, 2(4), e0000169. https://doi.org/10.1371/journal.pclm.0000169

Garel, A., Romec, A., Sautner, Z., & Wagner, A. F. (2024). Do investors care about biodiversity? European Finance Review, 28(4), 1151-1186. https://doi.org/10.1093/rof/rfae010

Johnson, O., Mete, G., Sánchez, F., Shawoo, Z., & Talebian, S. (2021). Toward climate-neutral heavy industry: An analysis of industry transition roadmaps. Applied Sciences, 11(12), 5375. https://doi.org/10.3390/app11125375

Stoll, P., Pauw, P., Tohme, F., & Grüning, C. (2021). Mobilizing private adaptation finance: lessons learned from the Green Climate Fund. Climatic Change, 167(3-4). https://doi.org/10.1007/s10584-021-03190-1

UNEP. (2025). Adaptation Gap Report 2025: Running on Empty. UNEP. https://www.unep.org/resources/adaptation-gap-report-2025

Conclusion

The machinery examined in this book was built quickly and at considerable expense. Disclosure regimes now bind most large companies in major jurisdictions. Classification systems define what qualifies as sustainable. Rating agencies score tens of thousands of issuers. Labeled debt has become routine, impact investing manages assets in the trillions, and carbon pricing covers roughly a quarter of global emissions across eighty instruments. Judged by institutional construction, the past decade has been remarkably productive.

Judged by effect on capital allocation, the record divides sharply. A consistent finding across these chapters is that mechanisms depending on voluntary participation have delivered less than their volumes suggest. ESG integration produces divergent ratings whose disagreement dilutes the price pressure it is meant to create. Portfolio decarbonization reduces measured financed emissions while transferring assets rather than retiring them. Labeled debt achieves pricing benefits of fifteen to twenty basis points that do not change project economics. Sustainability-linked instruments set targets that issuers expect to meet. Voluntary carbon markets have systematically rewarded cheap credits over credible ones. In each case the instrument functions as designed while the design is not equal to the claim made for it.

Mechanisms that apply regardless of preference have performed better where they have been applied. Carbon pricing produces measurable abatement in rigorously evaluated systems, with China's regional pilots delivering emissions reductions of nearly 17 percent among covered firms. Prudential supervision has changed how banks assess climate exposure. Engagement, unlike divestment, shows a documented association with reduced downside risk and fewer environmental incidents. The pattern is that instruments altering relative returns or carrying regulatory force outperform instruments relying on investors choosing to act.

The binding constraint is also clearer than it was a decade ago. Aggregate capital is not scarce; global climate finance reached USD 1.9 trillion in 2023 and continues to grow. What is scarce is capital willing to be deployed in the places and activities where the need is greatest, at a price those activities can pay. A climate vulnerability premium of over one percentage point on sovereign borrowing, an adaptation finance gap twelve to fourteen times current flows, and 2 percent of clean energy investment reaching a continent holding 20 percent of the world's population are all expressions of the same problem. It is a problem of risk pricing and public good financing, not of investor awareness, and the mechanisms that dominate sustainable finance address awareness.

This is not an argument that the architecture was wasted. Disclosure, taxonomies, and measurement standards are preconditions for everything else, and their absence would leave regulators without a basis for enforcement and investors without a basis for comparison. The error lies in treating preconditions as outcomes, and in reporting volumes of labeled capital as though volume were evidence of effect.

Acceleration, if it comes, will follow from a small number of changes rather than from further product innovation. Extending mandatory carbon pricing beyond a quarter of global emissions would alter relative returns across the unpriced remainder. Compressing the risk premium in developing economies, through guarantees, currency instruments, and expanded multilateral capacity, would move more capital than every voluntary mechanism combined. Directing public balance sheets toward adaptation and pre-commercial technology, rather than toward mature renewables that attract commercial financing unaided, would apply scarce concessional resources where nothing else works. Each requires political durability more than financial ingenuity.

The distinction that has organized this book is therefore also its conclusion. Some mechanisms change what is known about capital. Others change what capital costs and where it goes. The first category is now well developed. Whether the second grows to match it is the question on which the financing of the transition turns.

www.ingramcontent.com/pod-product-compliance
Lightning Source LLC
LaVergne TN
LVHW030728061126
851857LV00019B/2033
* 9 7 8 1 9 9 1 3 6 8 9 9 7 *